THE BABY FARM MURDERS

THE TERRIFYING CASE OF THE ANGEL-MAKER, AMELIA DYER

RYAN GREEN

For Helen, Harvey, Frankie and Dougie

Disclaimer

This book is about real people committing real crimes. The story has been constructed by facts but some of the scenes, dialogue and characters have been fictionalised.

Polite Note to the Reader

This book is written in British English except where fidelity to other languages or accents are appropriate. Some words and phrases may differ from US English.

YOUR FREE BOOK IS WAITING

CONTENTS

Terms, £10

Evelina Marmon had made a mistake. It was not an uncommon mistake for a woman to make. Women had been making that same mistake over and over since the dawn of time, which was somewhat lucky, given that it was the kind of mistake that meant that the human race kept on existing. But Evelina was not some cavewoman who could make this sort of mistake with no consequence. The year was 1896, and the initial mistake had happened around nine months ago when she'd met a charming young man while she was waiting at a bar in Cheltenham.

All night long, every time that he bought himself and his friends a drink, he'd drop a half penny for her to get a gin for herself. It was a long shift, and there were a lot of rounds being bought, and by the end of it all she was flushed and dizzy. In just the right state to make a mistake. As she closed the place up for the night, wiping down the tables, the man lingered. They chatted as she went, with him trailing around after her like a lost puppy, all the while still flattering her and charming her. She should never have gone with him when the doors were finally shut. She should never have followed him back to his lodging house, with her fingers threaded through his and the cool morning air doing nothing to cool off the heat that was building up inside of her. She'd made a mistake that night and when he'd been gone the next morning, she'd made up her mind that it wasn't the kind of mistake she could ever afford to make again. Imagine if she got a reputation for doing that sort of thing. She'd be out of work, tossed out of her lodging, and subsequently forced to do for money the very thing that she should never have done to start with.

It had been a hard-learned lesson that she planned to never revisit. She would exercise restraint and hold off until there was a wedding ring on her finger before she ever risked making that sort of mistake again, no matter how much she might have enjoyed it, or how natural it might have been. Animals were natural too, and you saw how they behaved, rutting in the streets. She was better than that. Better than nature. And when the next kindly smile turned her head, she would let it end with a gentle goodbye instead of facing the embarrassing and shameful possibility of waking in the cold bed of a stranger with no sign of him left behind save for a few stains on the rumpled sheets.

That should have been the end of it. She'd learned from her mistake. She'd gone to church full of sorrow over her sin. She didn't need any punishment to remind her that she had to do better.

And then the blood hadn't come.

Every month like clockwork she'd bled, ever since she was a girl. She was twenty-four by then, so it had been years enough for her to know when it was due, but instead of the cramps and the bleeding and rags bundled up between her legs making waiting tables even more of an awkward chore, there had been nothing at all. She'd discounted it. Maybe she'd miscounted, or maybe things were just running slow in her body that month. No cause for alarm. Something she might mention to her mother if she ever got a chance to sit down with her, but otherwise a fairly minor oddity.

Sex education was not a high priority in Victorian England. Education in general was considered to be wasted on women, and women of low breeding like Evelina weren't likely to have even seen the inside of a classroom in most cases. Besides, sex was one of the greatest taboos that there was. Nobody spoke about it, even amongst family members or close friends, for fear that showing any knowledge of it would imply things about their character. So everything that Evelina had learned was from whispers and rumours that didn't seem to make any sense. She certainly wouldn't have known any of the signs of pregnancy. That sort of knowledge was held only by the esteemed and well-educated doctors and passed down orally from midwife to midwife in the slums of the city.

You could argue that cities themselves were the trouble. Nobody who had grown up on a farm would have had any doubt about what happened after beasts lay together. By Evelina's age, a country girl had probably served as a midwife for some animals on the farm. But now that the populations of England were entirely concentrated in the cities, the people that dwelled there were entirely cut off from the natural order of things. All that they knew was what they'd been told, and nobody had told any of them a whisper about what it meant when your period stopped and you felt queasy every single morning.

It was the first time that Evelina had been pregnant in her life, and with her being so young, her body showed little signs of the pregnancy for months on end. She just assumed that she had some little stomach bug, and that was why she felt sick and bloated. It wasn't as though she could afford to visit a doctor and ask for help for something so minor. It wasn't as though her leg had fallen off, so she wasn't going to squander her hard-earned money on a visit to a hospital or a clinic.

Months rolled on by without Evelina having the slightest clue about what was growing in her womb. She forgot about the blood that used to come every month. Forgot about her dalliance with a charming boy that she never saw again. Life was hard enough without daydreaming about problems that didn't even exist, so why would she spend a moment dwelling on them when the next round had been ordered and there had been a spill in the back and the bottles needed wiped down and her boss was threatening to cut her pay if she dropped another glass.

That's the funny thing about life: it goes on. It doesn't matter how terrible a mistake you've made or what is happening beyond the limits of your perception and understanding, every day the sun rises, and the bills need paying. So she got up and went to work and the weight inside of her grew heavier and heavier without her even noticing it. The sickness passed and faded from her memory much as the bleeding had. Even the night that she'd done the one thing she was never meant to do faded away. Almost six months had gone by before one of the other girls in the bar pulled her aside and asked about her baby.

Evelina didn't know what she was talking about. She didn't have a baby, she wasn't even married, what was the girl trying to say? Even when the other waitress placed her hand on Evelina's stomach and the protruding curve that had appeared over the last few months, she still didn't put it together.

It was only as she lay in her bed that night, nestled in the dark listening to the snores and sobs of everyone else trying to make it through the night, that she finally understood the question. It wasn't because she'd worked out what the other girl was talking about or that she'd made the connection with her sordid encounter in another equally miserable boarding house. It was because the baby kicked.

She had felt movement before, of course she had, but there had always been more important things to focus on, real problems to deal with. A crate needing brought up from the basement. A few extra pennies she needed to scrabble for in tips so that she could make her rent. A hole in her shoe that needed to be cobbled. But now, as she lay entirely alone in the midst of the dark night, she was struck by an awful certainty, the astounding realisation that she was not alone at all. There was another person there, inside of her. A baby, a child that she was going to have out of wedlock.

Her life was over. Everything she'd worked for, everything she'd strived for, all the months and years of clawing herself up from the gutters, it was over. She was ruined. Nobody would hire her once she was sacked from the Cheltenham bar. Not once they knew she was a fallen woman. No respectable doss-house would give her a bed for fear that she might spread her harlot ways to their other residents or bring johns home with her and thereby transform the once-reputable establishment into nothing more than a common whorehouse. That baby would be like the mark of Cain on her, visible to all, damning her for eternity. There could be no coming back from this. She was ruined.

Her voice joined the others sobbing in the dark of the night, echoing back and forth between the paper-thin walls. Everything was ruined, and she had nobody to blame but herself. She hadn't been forced, she hadn't been tricked, she'd gone with that man and laid herself down and revelled in unbridled hedonism. This was the price that she had to pay. Complete destruction.

Evelina didn't sleep that night, her head spinning and aching with the awful realisation of what had happened to her, but with the coming of dawn came a new hope, too. She was not the only girl in the world who'd run into a problem like this. Victorian England was hardly deprived of women who had made mistakes, quite the opposite in fact. As the inevitable result of the complete lack of any reliable and medically safe means for terminating an unwanted pregnancy was available to the lower classes, a somewhat clandestine type of business emerged to provide an alternative. Such places that would take a baby and raise it so that nobody ever had to know who its parents were. Wealthy couples unable to have children of their own could then adopt such waifs born of ill fortune. There were so many whispered stories about such things that, surely, some part of the rumours had to be true.

She confided in the other waitress that day, confessing her sins and seeking absolution. As it happened, she never even needed to ask for it. The other girl was not so puritanical as everyone around them seemed to be, she didn't even question who the father of the child was or why they weren't wed. Instead, she offered up practical advice, woman to woman. The way that women have done since before history was recorded. Through her, Evelina found a midwife who could answer all her questions and point her in the right direction.

She would have the child because there was no subtle way of being rid of it now that things were so far along. No special tea that she could drink to make the problem disappear. No procedure that midwives weren't meant to know, but nonetheless did. She was assured that this was not the end of her life as she'd assumed. Most folks never even knew just how many babies were out there being born every day. Half the women that Evelina knew might have had one and she'd never have been any the wiser. It was all a matter of dressing right, timing things and keeping your mouth shut. So long as nobody knew with certainty that she was pregnant, so long as she wasn't carting a baby around with her, they'd never need to know. So long as the baby had somewhere to go, she might even be able to get it back in a few years once she had found some man to settle down with. Folks didn't pay all that much attention, especially in a big city like this. You could get away with far more than she'd ever realised if you kept to yourself and dealt with your problems in a sensible manner. But first thing was first, she had to have this baby.

There would be no hospital visit for young Evelina, just boiled water, fresh towels and the reassuring presence of the midwife by her side, talking her through everything as it happened.

The labour was not easy, because no labour is easy. A woman might forget afterwards just how awful things were, but that did not mean that the pain was not immense, that the exhaustion was not bone deep or that the fear was not overwhelming. It is in our nature to forget, otherwise we would only ever have a single child, but for most parents, there is something that helps with the forgetting. The baby itself. The bond that is formed, the love that develops, even the absolute adoration and pure wonder that most parents feel the first moment that they look at their child is part of the deep-abiding love that is hard-wired into our brains to ensure that the species goes on existing despite the fact that we spend our most vulnerable early years as little more than screaming meat lumps. But poor Evelina knew, even as she bled and tore and wept, that the baby would not be hers to keep. She would not have a lifetime with it. She would not be allowed to cradle it in her arms and rock it to sleep every night. All the things that make going through the awful trauma of giving birth worthwhile were going to be taken from her, and she had to come to terms with that in exactly the same moment that she was straining to bring new life into the world.

This was her baby. But it would not remain her baby. She would not be the one to raise it. To teach it to speak. To encourage its first steps. It would not know her face. In all likelihood, it would not even know her name. For all that she might have had dreams of that promised future when they would be reunited again under one roof, with some faceless father roped in so that the whole world would not turn against them, the truth was that more likely than not, her child was never going to know her.

The tears streamed down her face mingled with the sweat. If this had been her second or third child, it would have been long done by now. But this was her firstborn. Her first and only.

When the babe finally slipped free of her into the midwife's arms, she had lost track of how many hours had passed them by. It was all just one long horrible blur of motion and blood and pain. But now that the journey was done, the destination was so much sweeter. Wrapped up in the last clean towel in the whole boarding house, the midwife brought the tiny baby up to where Evelina lay, still too weak to move. She laid its head upon the mother's chest and let Evelina's heartbeat soothe the little one.

It was a girl, she told Evelina in what seemed like a distant whisper. A girl.

She called her Doris.

The first day after the baby was born, Evelina was basically left alone to get on with things. The midwife had given instructions on how to nurse the babe, how to fold a nappy, all the vital things to get through the first little while. Beyond that, she had been told to rest up for the time being. She'd thought that she would have spent the whole day with nobody for company but the baby. That the stigma around her would already have descended. To her amazement, every one of the girls that she worked with showed up with gifts and kind words, even the boss's wife who had made sure to keep her husband right the last few months when he started getting ideas about notions like sin and reputation. As much as she had wept over the baby coming to ruin her life, over the pain that she was suffering through, and the sorrow at the impending separation from her baby, nothing had made her sob and snivel like that kindness did.

All of them had known from the start, and none of them had said a word. None of them had looked down on her or cursed her name or cast her out, because but for a bit of bad luck, she could have been any one of them.

Society at large might have loathed single mothers, but when you broke that society down to individuals who actually knew the single mothers as people instead of an abstract concept, that level of contempt was impossible. In the big picture, tiny details could be missed but Evelina was never going to forget this kindness and she would never fail to pay it forward for the rest of her life. The modern Protestant mantra of hate the sin, love the sinner, may not have been circulated so much in Victorian England, but there were still kind and goodhearted people intent on doing the right thing regardless of what the baying masses thought.

They didn't coddle her, much as she might have appreciated it, but they did show her that the sky had not fallen, and the world had not ended. So long as she was able to deal with her little problem promptly and succinctly there would be a life still waiting for her on the other side.

And so, the very next morning she rose from the bed where she'd spent much of the last few days, and with her baby cradled in her arms she made her way over to the little table that served as both her dressing table and her writing desk. There she carefully jotted down her advertisement. 'Wanted, respectable woman to take a young child.' It would appear in the newspaper the next day in the miscellaneous section of the Bristol Times & Mirror. She received a copy of the paper to make sure that it had been printed correctly and was amazed to discover what looked like the answer to all her prayers just one column over.

'Married couple with no family would adopt a healthy child, nice country home. Terms, £10'

All the money she'd spent placing her advert, and the answer to all her problems was right there all along. She sent a letter along to 'Mrs Harding' the very same day, and by the end of the week, she had her reply.

"I should be glad to have a dear baby girl, one I could bring up and call my own. We are plain, homely people, in fairly good circumstances. I don't want a child for money's sake, but the company and home comfort. I and my husband are dearly fond of children. I have no child of my own. A child with me will have a good home and a mother's love."

It seemed like the perfect solution. A couple that wanted a child of their own and couldn't have one. A baby that needed a home. The only concern that dogged Evelina was that when she had her life together and came back for her daughter, she wasn't sure that this couple would be willing to give her up.

At the same time, she had no idea how to inform Mrs Harding that this was going to be a temporary situation without putting her off entirely. If this woman wanted a child of her own, to have and to hold, to love as if she'd given birth to it herself, then she was hardly going to want to give Doris back when all was said and done. They wrote back and forth a little more, discussing terms. £10 was not a ridiculous amount of money to give someone for taking care of your baby, but it was a massive amount for Evelina to secure in one lump sum. She'd heard from the other girls and the midwife that arrangements could usually be made where a weekly sum was paid over, which felt like a good way to keep her existence present in Mrs Harding's mind and to ensure that when the time came, she'd have some small degree of leverage to get her daughter back.

Unfortunately, Mrs Harding had no interest in a weekly payment, she wanted her full 10 pounds upfront. It seemed to be the only issue that was preventing them from coming to an arrangement. Yet presented with no better options for the care of her baby, eventually, Evelina was forced to concede and pay the full sum in advance.

The situation at home had gone from bad to worse. Her job was now being threatened, not due to the initial indiscretion or the subsequent shame of having a baby out of wedlock, but due to her absence.

With no one to care for the baby, she could hardly wait tables and the longer that the situation persisted the more that her meagre savings were depleted. Paying the 10 pounds would deplete them entirely of course, but at least it would allow her to return to work and make an attempt to make ends meet.

About a week after her concession, Mrs Harding arrived in Cheltenham. Evelina was immediately surprised by the woman's appearance. She had been expecting someone in her 30s, not the stocky old woman that presented herself. Yet despite Mrs Harding's stoutness and grim demeanour, Evelina found herself relaxing after seeing the obvious affection that the old woman displayed towards her daughter. In a way, perhaps this would be better. Little Doris would grow up thinking that she was staying with a grandmother or elderly relative so when the time came for

Evelina to reclaim her, there would be less confusion. For a time, they sat in that tiny room of her boarding house, tears pricking at Evelina's eyes all the while as they discussed the home that her daughter would be raised in. The husband who provided for everything that the old woman needed and more. The garden in which little Doris would be able to spend the summer months playing, chasing butterflies and gazing at the kind of pastoral beauty that Evelina herself had only seen glimpses of in old paintings.

The city was no place for a child to grow up. Far from nature and sunshine and joy. Doris would have the kind of life that Evelina had never had the chance to experience. The kind of life that she wished with all her heart that she could have lived. There was no greater gift that she could give to Doris than to get her away from all this. Away from whispers of her parentage, and the dismal state of affairs that had led to her creation. Far away from the crowds pressed in on all sides reeking of sweat and sorrow.

She deserved better.

With a breaking heart, Evelina handed over a cardboard box of clothes and the 10 pounds in cash. Yet even when she had done that, she discovered that when the time came to part from her baby, she could not untangle her arms from where they were wrapped around it.

Little baby Doris stared up at her with bright blue eyes looking like the very image of innocence. How anyone could look at this little life and think it a sin entirely escaped Evelina in that moment. This precious little creature was a miracle, and she would not let herself forget this moment. She would not forget the warmth of the baby in her arms or the demanding whistle of the train ready to depart, and to part them.

Try as she might, she could not let the baby go. She could not make herself want to let the baby go. This was her daughter. She was not a burden, she was not a curse and whatever shame might have rained down on her, surely Doris was worth that price.

Despite her stern expression, it was clear that Mrs Harding was not entirely without sympathy, so once they had arrived at the station and the moment came for them to separate with finality, she took Evelina by the arm and dragged her on board.

Evelina had followed Mrs Harding from her lodgings to Cheltenham station, and now on to Gloucester in a state of racked dismay. Only barely containing her sobs, she realised that she could not tear her eyes away from Doris' face.

This was her baby. The only thing in all the world that was truly hers. The only thing in all the world that she had ever truly loved. She had not even known that love was real until she held that baby in her arms. She had not even known that there was this entire hidden world of human experience behind the mean-spirited cruelty that characterised every moment of her own life.

More time. She would have paid ten pounds more for just another day with Doris. She had been so desperate to send her away, so desperate to be free of the burden and the fear of discovery, that it had not even crossed her mind that this moment when it came, would be so agonizing.

She needed those extra precious moments with her daughter on the train to make peace with what had to be done. To convince her grasping arms that they could release the baby into Mrs Harding's care. Rationally, she might have known what the best course was, but there was nothing rational about the tearing feeling in her chest. She had never known pain like this, not even when she had been laid up in her bed trying to push Doris out into the world.

It was the hardest thing that she had ever had to do, but for her baby, she was willing to do it. She forced her vice-like grip on the baby to loosen. She pressed a final kiss to the tip of Doris' button nose, and at Gloucester she climbed off the train, tears streaming down her face and her baby now gone.

Mrs Harding would carry on to Reading. To her husband and her home where little Doris would be raised.

But Evelina had no such comforts awaiting her. Her heart was broken. Her home was empty. The promised return to normalcy had lost all of its appeal.

In spite of herself and all good sense, Evelina had fallen in love. Not with the spectre of the man that she had barely crossed paths with, but with her own daughter.

She could feel her sorrow like a tight knot in her chest. She was possessed by the desperate need to rush back to the train station, to rescue her daughter from the clutches of the kindly old woman who had promised to care for her. To drag her back here, £10 or not, and live out all their days together no matter how miserable those days might become.

The only thought that let her overcome that urge was the knowledge that it would not just be herself that she was consigning to hell, but poor little Doris as well. Doris would grow up a whore's daughter with no better prospects for her own future. She would be shunned by all that looked upon her as the product of monstrous sin. With Mrs Harding, Doris had the chance at a real life, she could grow up far away from all this, she could grow up to be anything that she dreamed of being, supported by someone so desperate for a child to love that she would accept a stranger's child without any questions asked.

That day stretched out into the cold of night, and still Evelina sat on the end of her bed, staring at the empty basket where her daughter had slept. All the blankets had gone away with the baby girl, all her clothes, the little toys people had gifted, and every trace that Evelina ever had a daughter was now wiped away.

She was alone. Alone in a way that she had never been before. Like a sprouting seedling that had finally broken the surface of the earth and felt the warm touch of the sun, only for night to fall.

Before Doris, Evelina had been alone, lonely, unaware of life's possibilities. Now she knew better. Now she knew how life was meant to be, filled to bursting with love, and the absence of it was an agony she could not have comprehended.

All night she sat there, unmoving, feeling the pain. Distracting herself now and then with an imaginary future in which she was reunited with her daughter, and they somehow made up for this lost time. It was a wonderful dream, but it had always been merely a dream. She knew that now.

In her mind, she might have been able to conjure up these joyful scenarios in which she was reunited with Doris and they were able to go on and live a happy life. She could imagine finding a husband so understanding that he treated the girl as his own flesh and blood. She could imagine making so much money she could retire to the country and pretend to be a widow. The whole world might flip on its head, and a daughter born out of wedlock would cease to be a source of shame, and they could get a little room just like this one and spend all their days together. But her current state of mind was far less pragmatic than her heart, and in her heart of hearts, she knew the truth was that she would never see her daughter again.

This wasn't just the terrible depression that she was sinking into speaking to her. It wasn't just the dread of being parted from Doris for the first time in their lives. She felt it with an awful certainty. The time would never come that they could be together again. She would never find a husband, or make a fortune, or anything else. Nothing good had ever happened to her before Doris, and nothing good was going to happen now that she'd taken the one good thing in her whole life and thrown it away. Her heart ached, but her gut told her that they'd never be together again.

And she was right. Doris was already dead.

Pyle Marsh

Amelia Elizabeth Hobley was born in 1837, the youngest of five children in a relatively happy home. They lived in the village of Pyle Marsh, some few miles east of Bristol, well taken care of by their father Samuel Hobley, who was a master shoemaker of enough renown that the family could have been five times the size without struggling. Thomas, James, William and Sarah Ann had grown up in relative luxury for the time, with education and books freely available for them to read in a period when literacy was usually the preserve of the upper classes, and now Amelia joined them in that oddly elite group, as one of the few common folk in the village who could understand the written word.

It set her and her family apart from everyone else, isolating them socially to a degree, but it also made them an invaluable part of the community. Samuel was obviously well respected as a craftsman anyway, with people from all over the surrounding area coming to Pyle Marsh to peruse his wares and boosting the local economy as a result, but the fact that the family could be relied upon to help with matters of writing was what pushed them over the top in terms of social clout.

Offsetting this enviable social status, however, was the matter of their mother, Sarah.

During the Great Irish Famine there had been a major epidemic of Typhus which had spread to areas of England, and as a part of the unwashed masses of the lower classes, Sarah had been exposed to it. There was no known treatment for the louse-borne disease at the time, with antibiotics not being widely available until the following century, and while the bacterial infection did not succeed in killing the woman, it did result in permanent brain damage.

Sarah's resultant mental illness and violent fits were the first things to poison Amelia's childhood, but they would be far from the last.

Despite all of the care with which Samuel treated his children, he seemed to have something of a blind spot when it came to his wife. He would leave them in her care despite her mercurial mood swings and erratic behaviour, perhaps simply because he had no other option if he meant to go on with his life. While the older children quickly learned how to navigate their mother's behaviour, Amelia, being the youngest, was often left stuck in the house with her during even her most chaotic outbursts.

In 1841, Sarah Ann, the eldest daughter of the family died of a longstanding illness leaving young Amelia to inherit the majority of 'womanly' duties around the household. It had long been realised that Sarah was incapable of keeping the house on her own, but with the assistance of her young children, things could be kept in a somewhat reasonable state. As the boys grew older, however, and began developing their own interests, they drew away more and more. They would abandon the house from sun-up to sunset in an effort to avoid the myriad responsibilities they never should have been burdened with and that, unfortunately, left poor little Amelia to pick up the slack. She was only four years old when her older sister died and she was immediately expected to take over the cooking and cleaning, not to mention running about town on household errands. Amelia, being a delicate child, must have suffered an incredible shock when, within the span of a week, she was abruptly confronted with the grim reality of human mortality in addition to suddenly finding herself saddled with all the duties of adulthood. It is a testament to the child's good temperament and precocious nature that she was able to cope with even a fraction of the duties she had inherited as a result of the untimely death of her sister.

And just when she felt that she was beginning to get a handle on things, just as it seemed like life might slip back into some semblance of stability, her mother fell pregnant again.

Sarah had already been next to useless, and now they had to contend with trying to keep the house in order, and keeping her calm so that no harm befell her or the unborn baby. The tightrope that the children had been walking all their lives had now narrowed down to a single thread, and poor little Amelia, who had barely learned to walk, was expected to navigate across the dark ravine of all the terrible things that could happen.

The doctor ordered Sarah to bed for extended periods of time during the pregnancy. It was not uncommon that for weeks or months at a time she would be sequestered in her dimly lit room, shouting out to her children whenever a fleeting fancy passed through her mind. If they dared to ignore her shrill demands they ran the risk of her emerging, putting herself and the baby at risk, not to mention endangering every one of them should the woman manage to lay hands on them. It did not matter which child had ignored her, whichever one she reached first would suffer the consequences. More often than not, that meant that Amelia, who had been rushing to her mother's aid as fast as her little legs could carry her but hadn't made it quite in time, became the unfortunate recipient of her mother's fits of wrath.

Perhaps because of her relative youth and immaturity, or perhaps because she had been so taken with the poetical and romantic, it seemed that Amelia never truly saw her mother's condition for what it was. She internalised the abuse that she suffered at her mother's hands when the woman succumbed to one of her bouts of madness and rationalised it as a well-deserved punishment for her own poor behaviour. It was her fault if she hadn't been fast enough to help mother to the bathroom, so, of course, she was to blame for the resulting mess. She was to blame if she hadn't been there when her mother needed a cup of tea made, so of course she deserved to have the hot spoon pressed into her arm. There was an endless cavalcade of minor tortures inflicted on the little girl each and every day by her mother, who often didn't realise what she had done until long afterwards when any attempt to apologise or explain herself would have been an utter waste even had she recalled any details from her violent episodes.

Her brothers were supposed to be there to help her along through all of this, but neither one had any interest in playing nurse to their frightening mother. Thomas was of an age now that he could join his father in the shop and learn the cobbling trade. The other two brothers alternated between roaming around the village and surrounding countryside for their own amusement and idly loafing around the house, both of which created more demands on little Amelia, who they had begun to treat less like a sibling and more like a servant.

In spite of everything, a little sister was born in 1845. Amelia was eight years old by this point, in charge of the cooking and cleaning around the house, as well as organising the boys into something resembling a family unit to be present at important occasions such as this, though the latter task often seemed more onerous than the first.

It was not that their father did not care about them or could not see the strain that the situation was putting them under, it was more that he had no idea how to handle it himself. He had no experience with keeping a house, no more than Sarah would have known how to mend a punctured leather sole. And more than that, if he were to acknowledge his wife's illness and take some steps towards making life stable for his children, then he would likely have felt compelled to see it through to the end. And the only end for a woman in Sarah's condition was the bedlam house. She was incurably insane, and there was nothing that any amount of comfort or ease would do to change that.

There is also a strong likelihood that he was unaware of just how bad the situation was, because of how hard everyone else in his family was working to keep the awful truth hidden. They all knew that even mentioning Sarah's eccentricities was enough to turn their usually cheerful father sober and drawn, so they simply avoided talking about it. But just because a mental health problem is concealed does not mean that it doesn't exist, and the act of keeping it concealed often exacerbates the situation. What was already a major problem in their lives became an all-consuming one.

With the arrival of the new baby, named Sarah Ann in remembrance of the older sister that she'd never know, there came a period of deceptive peace and calm about the Hobley household. Carried along in a post-partum bliss, Mother Sarah drifted through the house like some benevolent spirit, doing little to help Amelia with all the chores that she had accrued, but no longer serving as an active hindrance to them all living their lives. The boys began to return home earlier and earlier in the day, taking their reading up once more now that they felt safe in the home. Much to Amelia's surprise, they would actually help her with the most difficult tasks she had to deal with, without complaint or asking. It had never been cruelty that had led them to abandon her, but the situation with their mother. The fires were set without her needing to go and cut wood. The table was set without her having to polish silverware. Once in a while it even seemed that a room had been swept without her having to sweep it.

For a time, it felt almost like they were a normal family again. Her mother, bouncing the baby on her hip, would sometimes be in the kitchen cooking dinner before Amelia had even gotten around to starting it. Her father would come home at a reasonable time from work before he'd driven himself to such exhaustion that he was guaranteed to sleep through whatever occurred in the night.

As fate would have it, like every moment of happiness that the Hobleys experienced, it was fleeting. The spectre of Sarah Hobley's madness was always there, like a curse, as if the infamous sword of Damocles loomed over them awaiting the first opportunity to drop down and sever the tenuous connection between this family and any sense of happiness or normalcy.

Only five months after the baby was born, that sword dropped and the Hobley's world fell to ruin once again. One morning all was quiet in the nursery, and suspecting that her mother had slept in again, Amelia crept in to check on the baby. Her mother was already there, sitting on the floor beside the bassinet. The baby in her arms, cold and unmoving. She was trying to nurse it despite rigour mortis already having set in, twisting its hardened limbs aside and trying to force her nipple into a mouth that was locked shut. Sarah hushed the silent baby time and again, and Amelia could do nothing but stand and stare.

Eventually, the girl had to run all the way into the village to fetch her father back, having no idea what to do with the grisly scene that was laid out before her. At scarcely nine years old, she did not yet have a firm grasp on mortality or on madness. She could not have fully understood what she was really looking at.

It would only be after her father had returned home and pried the dead baby from his wife's arms that sound seemed to return. An awful, unholy wailing, so loud and animalistic that you could scarcely believe that it was coming from the mouth of a human being. Yet it was her mother, screaming and sobbing and wailing. Attacking her husband to try and get the dead baby back from him, as though it had been him that had stolen it from her rather than death itself.

It would never be known what actually killed the second Sarah Ann Hobley. Whether it was simple cot death as the villagers came to believe, or if something far darker had occurred during one of her mother's fits. No examination of the baby was carried out by a doctor, and she was laid to rest in the village graveyard as swiftly and silently as was possible.

Regardless of the cause, the result was immediately visible.

Whatever minimal mask of sanity Sarah Hobley had managed to hold up all these years had now been irrevocably fractured. Whether the death of her daughter had shattered what little remained of her sanity after the ravages of typhus or if she simply no longer felt the need to maintain her guise as a normal mother given the absence of her child, the net result was the same. She degenerated entirely into madness, losing all capability of caring for herself or others. Where before poor Amelia had been tasked with filling in the gaps and cracks in her parents' marriage and household, now she assumed the full role of the mother. All of the cooking and cleaning now fell entirely into her domain. All the running of the household, the bills, the shopping, everything that in a reasonable world would have been handled by an adult was now tackled exclusively by this child. A child, it should be noted, who had just gone through the terrible trauma of witnessing the death of one of her siblings.

Incredibly, it was not only the care of her mother's children and household that fell to young Amelia, but the care of her mother as well, given the woman was now utterly incapable of caring for herself. Sarah no longer got out of bed. She could no longer dress herself. Bathing was a distant memory. And when she did drag herself out to wander the town, she was a source of dreadful shame for the Hobley family. Amelia became her keeper. She was tasked with keeping up appearances despite the impossibility of the trials that lay before her. There was far too great a disparity in their size and age for Amelia to effectively manage her mother's state of disrepair and complete disregard for appearances. She could not force her mother to bathe, though in her less lucid moments, Sarah could be bathed by the child. It was a terrible thing for Amelia to wish that her mother was catatonic, but the sad fact of the matter was that she was considerably easier to manage as a vegetable than as a rambling mad woman.

Yet beyond the oppressive prison walls of what should have been their beloved family home, life did still go on. Her brothers were trained under her father, in apprenticeships. Amelia pursued such education as she could, given the constraints with which she was fettered. Even their father pressed on with his profession drawing as much, if not more, acclaim for his work despite the dire circumstances. He had always escaped from the nightmare of his home into the sanctuary of his work. As his wife had transformed before his eyes from the woman that he had fallen in love with into some sort of grotesque facsimile that bore the same face but with none of the same person behind it, he spent more and more time at the shop. Leaving Amelia to handle everything.

William and Martha Hobley were Amelia's aunt and uncle, living in close proximity, but providing shocking little aid to the poor girl.

This should have come as no surprise really, given that they were Samuel's family and, therefore, received all news about the family and home from Samuel, himself, who continued to live in a state of perpetual denial. He told them that everything was alright, and they believed him. Though rumours swirled through the village about the degeneration of Sarah Hobley, William and Martha were the first to deny such rumours. Surely they, of all people, would be the first to know if something so terrible had occurred following the death of little Sarah Ann. Samuel insisted that all was well, so why would they ever doubt his word regardless of the village scuttlebutt. The united front presented by William, Martha and Samuel was actually one of the few things that was holding back the tide of public opinion about Sarah. All three of them were respected members of the community and so long as they remained so, there was never going to be any intervention into the private affairs of the Hobley household. For as long as the illusion could be maintained, if they could manage to preserve their respectability, the village of Pyle Marsh was certainly not going to be allowed to strip it from them by force.

But of course, the world was not so perfect as they liked to pretend. Scandal would soon find William and Martha Hobley just as surely as Sarah's madness would be discovered.

They had a daughter who proved to be less virtuous and upstanding than the Hobley uncle and aunt might have hoped. She returned home from the big city with a distinctive swell to her stomach that in a married woman would have been cause for celebration but in a young allegedly innocent girl was possibly the greatest scandal that could have descended upon them.

Once again, things happen behind closed doors. The illegitimate child of their daughter was born in privacy with only a midwife in attendance who had been sworn to secrecy. For a time, cries of the baby could be heard from outside of their home yet polite neighbours would swear that they could hear nothing at all. When the babe did finally make its debut into society, it was introduced as being Martha's rather than her daughter's. And like a great many of the polite little lies that had to be believed for society to continue to function, this rather feeble deception was accepted, unquestioned.

Whatever excitement such scandal might have brought, passed Amelia by entirely. When she was a little girl reading her books, the world had seemed so vast, so full of wonders and distant places awash with their exotic draw. But as time had gone by, her world had shrunk. First, it became the size of the village and all her dreams had to be crushed down and contained within the one-mile marker on the roads out of town. Then it had become smaller still, the family home, the village store, the odd outing to bring a forgotten parcel of lunch to her father or brothers. Now it became no larger than the house itself. She was a prisoner of her mother's sickness. Sarah could not be left alone, not safely, and not for any length of time. It was not so much that she was a danger to herself deliberately, but more that she had completely forgotten how to function and as such was liable to do herself harm in the most foolish of ways. Falling down the stairs, burning herself on the fire, drowning herself in the water barrel, none of these were beyond reason. During her worse bouts before, she had been purposefully self-destructive but now it seemed she lacked even the capacity to wish harm on herself. There was no intent behind these brushes with danger and death. Only a vacant nothingness behind her eyes. Amelia came to long for the days when her mother used to scream and shout and tear clumps of her own hair out when she used to chase her children around the house threatening to tan their hides if she caught them. At least when she was playing the monster, it showed that there was someone inside of Sarah's body. It may not have been the mother that they wanted or needed, but at least someone was there. More often than not, Amelia felt that she was entirely alone within the house. There may have been another body there, groaning and moaning and moving around, but there was nobody inside it. Even an animal would have been better company.

This grim state of affairs continued for three years, from the death of Sarah Ann in 1845 to the death of her mother in 1848. The exact circumstances of Sarah's passing remain unknown to us although it is somewhat inevitable that Amelia would have been present for the event itself given that she spent every waking moment in her mother's company, doing her best to keep the woman alive. The cause of death was listed as complications from typhus, which technically is true even if the specifics of these complications are lost to us. Regardless, it marked the end of Amelia's servitude and imprisonment in the family home, and she was quick to take advantage of it. With her father's permission and blessing, she left the village of Pyle Marsh to take up an apprenticeship with the corset maker in Bristol and found lodgings with a dowager aunt who lived in the city.

Her relationships with other women were shaped by her experiences with her mother. Were she not so blatantly subservient to everyone, in all likelihood she would have been considered quite manipulative given how she always said exactly what she thought the person she was speaking to wanted to hear. It may have been a holdover from her youth of placating a mad woman, but after years of having been trapped in close proximity to someone who had no real sense of reality, Amelia seemed to have developed a rather fluid relationship with the truth. She did not hesitate to say whatever she felt needed to be said to get what she wanted or to simply get by with the minimum amount of friction. Her aunt was elderly enough that this behaviour went mostly unnoticed, given the old woman's own faltering faculties. But in the workplace, it left her with few friends among the other apprentices and the reputation of someone inclined to make false promises that they could not fulfil with her employer. There had been some who hoped that she might have inherited her father's talents and would be capable of applying them to a new craft but it seemed that she lacked a great many things that had made her father special. In fact, in many ways she seemed to be a counterpoint to him, where he had excelled thanks to his nature as a perfectionist constantly driving him to do the finest work possible, Amelia's attitude was considerably more lax. If given the opportunity to slack off from work, she would take it quite happily. If given the option to cut a corner, she would cut it. It was as if her predilection for seeking the path of least resistance in conversation was equally applied in her approach to work. The other factor that had greatly contributed to her father's great success as a shoemaker was his relentless work ethic. He would continue to push himself to his limits each and every day both in terms of quality and quantity of goods produced. Meanwhile, Amelia was firmly of the opinion that she was paid the same regardless of whether she made a hundred corsets or one. She could see no benefit to working herself to the bone to enrich someone else. If there was no immediate advantage to her, then she had no interest.

She continued to bob along in this manner for a number of years until 1859 when she received word that her father, who seemed to have spent her entire adult life in mourning, had finally passed away and become the subject of mourning himself.

She returned to Pyle Marsh the same day the news arrived, abandoning her work and her aunt with scarcely a word of explanation. For all these years she felt that she'd been treading water waiting for her real life to begin, and now with whatever inheritance had been bequeathed to her with the passing of her father, she might finally be able to find a place for herself in the world. She had done so much for Samuel Hobley while he lived. She had carried his burdens when no one else could. She had taken on all the challenges that he himself should have faced so that he could go on banging away at his shoes quite contentedly as their whole world fell apart. In short, Amelia felt quite strongly that, clearly, she was owed a debt of gratitude from her dead father and when the time came for the reading of his will, it would finally be repaid in full.

For the past few years, working as an apprentice corset maker and handing over most of her meagre income to her aunt for her lodgings, she had been living like a church mouse with barely two pennies to rub together. All the while her father and brothers, seemingly oblivious to her life of hardship, were sitting on a small fortune back in Pyle Marsh. At long last, she would get a taste of that wealth, she would be able to return to the sort of life that she had been accustomed to before her mother had fallen into a pit of madness and despair.

As was to be expected, her eldest brother Thomas inherited the family shoe business. He had been training since he was old enough to walk on his own to take over the shoemaking business after their father's passing, so it hardly came as any great surprise. He may not have been able to match his father's mastery of the trade but he had learned as much as he could from the old man and he now set about sharing that hard-earned knowledge with his siblings who worked alongside him in the hope that even if he never achieved the same level of expertise in shoemaking as Samuel had reached, perhaps one of the others might be able to elevate their skill to the level of their father's art. And if not them, perhaps one of their many sons, or their many grandsons yet to come.

All her brothers had married in the intervening years, being free from the dark shadow of the mother's illness, and they had pressed on with their lives while Amelia seemed to have stalled. For the most part, the three brothers had remained close-knit, no longer sharing a home, but maintaining all the bonds of family that one would have expected. All of them except Amelia who had been essentially cast out on her own into the unforgiving city without a penny in her pockets or any legacy of success she could parlay into any form of social advancement. All three boys, now grown men, had followed in the father's footsteps in terms of their chosen profession. While Thomas had worked with their father, Samuel, both James and William had acquired cobbler's shops of their own in nearby villages. They were safe in the knowledge that if ever things did go wrong for them, there would always be a place for them here. A safe retreat from the difficulties of the world and a place where they could go back to honing their trade without any judgment or ill-treatment.

Amelia would have had no use for a cobbler's shop even if there had been the possibility of her receiving it, the business had never been what she wanted, just the benefits of it. The money that she knew her father had been piling away throughout the decades as the result of his acclaim and success. The boys could have the future that their father laid out for them, Amelia didn't want that future, she wanted freedom. Not the passing glimpses of it that she'd seen since escaping from under her mother's yoke, but true freedom to do as she pleased, to go as she pleased, to live life on her own terms instead of those that her parents had proscribed. Her inheritance would give her that at last. There were many things that women could not do in Victorian England, but wealth seemed to break down a great many barriers.

She looked around at her brother's wives with pity. For they were in bondage, forced to marry the first man that came along who might offer them a prospect at a stable life. Despite it all, despite all that she'd suffered and seen, in her heart of hearts Amelia remained a romantic. With her inheritance secured, she would be able to do the unthinkable. She would be able to marry for love if it so pleased her. She would be able to see those far-off places that she'd imagined as a child reading books by candlelight and pretending not to hear her mother's rantings. This money would be the making of her. It would be a new beginning, freed from the trappings of her previous servitude and sorrow.

The boys had run and hid when confronted with the awful reality of their mother's condition. It was Amelia who had been left behind to bear every burden, to suffer every insult and to scrape dried shit from the bedsheets on those days when Sarah was not even lucid enough to squat over her bedpan. But at last, finally, with her father's passing, she was going to be repaid the debt that all of them owed her.

The family home in Pyle Marsh would also pass to Thomas with the expectation that he would use it, or whatever revenues he gained from its sale for the advancement of the family business. If they meant to keep it on as a home and move their own families in then any of the brothers were welcome to do so, and it took barely a moment before such discussions began.

All the while, Amelia sat waiting. She did not care who received a cottage in some backwater village. She didn't care which of the boys had a bigger family that could make use of the space.

She was still waiting to hear what had become of the money.

All those years living with her parents Amelia had never understood that her father had sunk every penny of earnings into the house, the shop, the apprentices, and the business. There was not a sixpence that wasn't tied up in one or the other. The sacks of gold that she had been imagining hidden under her father's bed did not exist. The bountiful wealth that she had so long been craving to use to escape from the life she had lived in Pyle Marsh was all tied up in Pyle Marsh.

It would take until considerably later the in the proceedings for Amelia to finally reach this realization, by which point it had already been decided that as Thomas intended to remain in the village, he should be the one to inherit the family home. In a panic, Amelia demanded her money outright. She did not care if they kept the house, but to her thinking, she was entitled to a quarter share of whatever it should have sold for. There were three of them all well-established in their businesses, it should have been a simple matter for them to raise the funds necessary to buy her out of her quarter.

It is difficult to say whether confusion or dismay ruled in that room after she had said her part. All three brothers were close, close enough that the matter of money had not even entered into their minds. Much like their father, their businesses were not merely a means to an end for them, but an end in themselves. And as such, the part of shoemaking where you turn a profit rather than some leather never really entered into their minds. And just as money meant nothing to them because they had never been wanting for it, the very idea of something so tawdry entering into discussion on the day of their father's funeral was galling to them.

There had been a rift in the Hobley family stretching all the way back to their early childhood when Amelia, by virtue of her gender, was assumed to be perfectly content with her lot in life caring for all the others. It had never occurred to any of the boys that she did the things that she was forced to do out of a sense of filial duty rather than out of a desire to spend her time pottering around the house cleaning up after them. They had assumed that as a woman she was quite content with 'woman's work' when, in truth, seeing them go on with their lives and seeking contentment as she slaved away had created a truly bitter core within Amelia. The glaring inequity of her situation had birthed a simmering resentment that she had never been truly able to set aside even during those brief periods when her brothers were doing everything in their power to make her life easier. But of course, much like their father had been willfully unaware of so many of the troubles at home, so too were the boys. In truth they had never really given Amelia much thought, they had never recognised her growing resentment or even that she might have any reason for it. Amelia's childhood had been a torturous misery, but it was quite different for the boys. To their minds, despite being marked by their mother's illness, childhood was still a time fondly remembered. As such, when Amelia began speaking of debts due and the unfairness of all things, they were shocked and appalled that the sweet young girl that they recalled had turned into such a money-grubbing monster who, on the very day of their father's funeral, came clawing for whatever wealth she could scavenge. They may have been unaware of the rift between them before, but now the difference between their lives was markedly apparent. And for the crime of living in a world where comfort was not a given, they turned on her.

Confusion and horror gave way to anger, and all three of the brothers shouted Amelia down. How dare she come here making demands when she had abandoned the family the very moment that their mother's body was cold? When her father had been the most desperately in need of comfort? Only to turn and find his daughter, his most beloved child, wanted nothing more to do with him. When the Hobley family had needed her the most, she had fled to Bristol, to her new life that she had been so desperate to begin.

Needless to say, with three of them and only one of her, Amelia had no chance of successfully contesting the will. There was just no way for her to win. After everything that she had done for her family, the only payment that she would receive would be their scorn and contempt.

Of the three brothers, the one who benefited the most from the current arrangement was of course Thomas, who stood to inherit essentially everything that Samuel had spent his whole life working towards. As such, he became the greatest defender of the status quo and the primary focus of all Amelia's ire. While she may have felt the other two were complicit, Thomas was the one that she marked as her enemy. That being the case, he was the one to receive the sharp end of her tongue. She was a well-read young lady and had spent a great deal of time among the lower-class working folk of Bristol, so the things that she called her brother that day were not only terrible but offered a rather shocking and broad expansion of his vocabulary.

The family did not part on amicable terms, Amelia departed the village before the day was out, taking a train back to Bristol and her aunt who knew next to nothing of what had transpired back in Pyle Marsh. When the young woman arrived in the blackest of moods, the old widow assumed that it was a product of her grief. It would not be until almost a week later, a week during which the amicable and acquiescent Amelia had entirely transformed into a surly and snarling parody of herself, that a letter to the aunt would arrive from Amelia's eldest brother explaining with no small amount of hyperbole what had transpired in the week of their father's departure from the mortal coil.

As politely as it was possible to do so, Amelia's aunt and landlady for the past eleven years, asked the younger woman to pack her bags and find somewhere else to rest her head. Thomas was now the de facto leader of the whole Hobley clan, and no matter what personal connection Amelia's aunt may have felt to her, she was not willing to sever ties with the rest of her family just to protect the one black sheep.

Amelia, Alone

Cast out of the family home, Amelia bounced from one place to the next, moving from one doss house to another as she sought more permanent lodgings. Life had never been easy for her, but she was entirely unprepared for how difficult it would be to exist as a woman alone in the world of Victorian England. She could trust no one and was trusted by no one in turn. With her aunt and family behind her, she had at least been favoured with the appearance of some respectability even if her choice to strike out on her own, rather than staying home as would have been proper, was still questionable. In her new circumstances, devoid of any ties to a respectable family, it was now assumed she was a low woman, cast out for some sin and, therefore, a suitable punching bag for all of society. The life that she had lived as an apprentice corset maker had been far from luxurious, but now that she had to contend with the extortionate price of lodgings in comparison to the relatively fair deal that she had been receiving from her aunt, things went from bad to worse. The less money that she had, the shoddier the lodgings she had to seek, the shoddier her lodgings were, the more disrespectable she appeared, and so the downward spiral continued.

All that she needed to get back on her feet was a small injection of cash, a meagre stipend from her family would have made all the difference. But at the funeral, she had burned many bridges. Extended family would not reply to her letters, even as the desperation within them became more evident. It was difficult to strike a sympathetic figure and repair her reputation as a good and devoted daughter rather than a money-grubbing leech when in every letter she was essentially begging for money.

The real trouble for Amelia was that she had spent so much of her youth bound up in her duties that she'd never really had the opportunity to bond with any of her family. As a result of the dutiful care she provided for her mother, she had always been a background figure rather than a lead player on the stage of life. Consequently, she was mostly forgotten, known only through the tales that her brothers told of her. Tales which now painted her in a rather unflattering light.

Yet while she may have been entirely unaware of it, she did still have one member of the Pyle family on her side, serving as a spokesman and counselling moderation to those brothers whose tempers had flared. James was the middle of the three brothers and the least headstrong. It had been him, more often than not, that had helped around the house while his little brother, William, went off playing and his elder brother, Thomas, was consumed by his studies at the cobbler's shop. As such, he was probably the only one of the Hobleys who'd ever spent much time in Amelia's company. While the other two may have remembered her as less of a little sister and more like a maid figure doing the many chores around the house, James had spent time in that "maid's" company as she performed a myriad of household duties. He had known the sweet little girl that she had been before the misery of her life had ground that aspect of her away. He still thought of her as a person, something that was tragically revolutionary at the time, and he recognised that her demands for payment were not entirely unjust given how much she had sacrificed for them in their youth.

Out of everyone that Amelia had written to beseeching help, not once had it occurred to her to reach out to James. In her mind, he was just an extension of Thomas, in the camp of her enemy, so there was no point in attempting to make contact. He might have remembered her fondly, but her own recollections of the time placed him with the other two, ignorant of her suffering, ready to abandon her to her onerous tasks, and generally contemptible.

And of course, given her unstable housing situation, it was entirely impossible for him to send a letter to her given that he did not even know where she was.

It would only be after a full year that he would encounter one of the many letters that she had been sending out in desperation to the broader family. From it, he retrieved an address where he hoped she might still be reached. Unfortunately, it arrived too late at the lodging house where she had been staying, but thanks to some luck, it made its way to her through some of the friends she had been making in low places.

The two conducted a correspondence that would stretch out until 1861 with Amelia beseeching him to send her some portion of the family fortune so that she might survive, and James being entirely incapable of doing so given that it was still all tied up in property and their businesses. The only way that the Hobley fortune could be liquidated and shared with her would be through the consent of the other two brothers, both hard-headed men now that they were grown, and thoroughly disinclined to do anything to help their miserable shrew of a sister.

It took some time, but eventually, Amelia recognised that her brother was not lying to her or trying to trick her out of what she was due but was in fact doing all that he could to assist her. When he was able, he sent along some small amounts of money that he was able to secure for himself without the rest of the family noticing. This had stalled her descent into abject poverty for the immediate future, but there was nothing more that he could do without getting at least one of the other brothers on his side.

It was not going to be Thomas. Since the funeral, his opinion of Amelia had continued to decline. With every story that he heard from the extended family about her travelling around with a begging cap in her hands, the greater his contempt for her grew. Until finally he had reached the point where even the mention of Amelia's name was enough to drive him into a dark mood. Given his importance within the family, this resulted in a situation where almost everyone behaved as though Thomas had no sister, or that she had passed on the same day as their father. Discussed only in the past tense.

Due to Thomas' overt antipathy toward Amelia, James approached William, the youngest brother, to try and win him over to Amelia's cause. As it turned out, this was not a good decision. As he tried to sway William, he inadvertently let slip just how much he had been giving away to their wayward sister. While Thomas may have mastered dark moods and sulking as a means of dissuasion, William lacked the gravitas required to silently and sullenly still a room. His emotional state was expressed much more explosively. On learning that James had been quietly embezzling funds out of his own family's pockets to fund the cushy life of lazing around that they imagined Amelia was engaged in, he flew into a rage, screaming at his brother and bringing the whole family to weigh in on the matter.

Even James' own wife had been unaware of the money that he was taking from the business to fund his charitable donations. She was so caught up in William's wrath that it didn't seem to occur to her even once that perhaps her husband had the right of it, and the family should have been supporting the sister that they now all spurned. Yet even in the face of the entire family shouting him down, James showed remarkable resilience and stuck to his guns. He believed that Amelia needed their help. He believed that they owed it to her after the way that she had cared for them in their youth, even if everyone else was so quick to forget the way that their young sister had selflessly given so much of her own life so that they might enjoy theirs.

If he had thought that he could guilt the men into handing over a single penny to Amelia, then he was sorely mistaken. They were the wronged parties. They were the ones whom Amelia had insulted and sneered at just for doing exactly what their father had expected of them, growing up, working hard, and moving past the troubles of the past. It was Amelia who insisted on clinging to every little inconvenience as though it were a personal affront. As though having a mad woman for a mother hadn't been difficult for all of them. Yet while they had moved on with their lives and made something of themselves, she chose to wallow in self-pity and sorrow. They were not the problem here, she was, and if she expected them to financially support her just because she couldn't be bothered to learn a trade or marry someone suitable, then she was entirely out of luck.

Still, James held his ground. He would not abandon his sister even if the others were too pig-headed to show her a little compassion. Through all of William's ranting, Thomas had watched silently, weighing both arguments as though he were the arbiter of justice. He clearly considered himself to be the Solomon of the family, given the solution that he suggested in the end when all the bickering was done.

They would present Amelia with an ultimatum, two choices, two paths to follow. If her situation was truly as dire as she claimed, then she was welcome to return to Pyle Marsh. The family home that she had grown up in still stood, and there was room enough there for her to live comfortably as a part of Thomas's family. If she did not wish to be a part of the Hobley family anymore, they would gather what they could into a lump sum and send it to her on the condition that it would be the last communication that she had from anyone in the extended family for the remainder of her days.

One way or another this would prove either James or William correct. If, as James said, Amelia truly wanted to be part of the family once more, they would all welcome her home with open arms and care for her as though there had never been any dispute at all. But if she took the money, then that was proof that money had been all that she was seeking all along and whatever few pounds they managed to scrape together for her would be a small price to pay to be rid of her permanently.

Amelia took the money. She would never speak to a member of her family again and on those rare occasions in Bristol when she saw her aunt, she acted as though the old woman was invisible. If that was the price that had to be paid to get what she deserved, then she would pay it gladly.

In 1861, now aged 24, Amelia finally had what she thought she had wanted all through her childhood. Just enough financial stability that she did not need to marry some beastly man simply to keep a roof over her head. She found herself a permanent room in lodgings on Trinity Street in Bristol, a better class of place than she'd ever been able to secure before but not a place in which she received no scrutiny. She was still young, pretty, and unattached, all of which came with a degree of suspicion about her morals. Surely by the lofty age of 24, she should have been married. It was not as though there was a shortage of bachelor's in Bristol.

Amelia kept to herself for the most part, something that was viewed with a great deal of suspicion at the time. Most women would have been in a desperate frenzy seeking a husband before they became an old maid and all chances at a decent life passed them by. Amelia, however, seemed to be absent of this fear. She was considered a suspect because she seemed quite content with her life alone.

But as often happens with love, it came to her when she least expected it and had not even considered going looking for it.

One of the many signs that the home in Trinity Street was not the most high-class of boarding establishments was the fact that it allowed both unmarried male and female residents. They were not permitted the sordid impropriety of sharing rooms or even going inside the rooms of those of the opposite gender, but that did not mean they didn't cross paths in the communal areas and get to know one another in that way. After so many years of being looked on as nothing more than a pretty prize by men her own age, Amelia was careful to keep a distance from them and the complex relationship that she had with other women prevented her from forming many friendships there, either. Somehow, George Thomas managed to slip entirely past all her defences.

Amelia was 24 and George was 59, 35 years her senior and more than old enough to have been her father. He had lived a long and lonely life, bereft of any great romance or even the company of the fairer sex beyond a few brief dalliances in his youth that had never gone far. By this stage in his life, he'd entirely given up on the idea of ever finding a wife and settling down, hence his ongoing tenancy in Trinity Street. There was no wife waiting at home to make his dinner after a hard day's work, so he was happy to pay a little extra money beyond the usual cost of renting a room at the boarding house in exchange for board. He fully intended to live out the remainder of his days as a bachelor and someday be taken from his room to be laid to rest in a potter's field.

It was to their immense mutual surprise that Amelia and George hit it off immediately, sharing newspapers at the breakfast table and chattering about their contents while most of the household was still groggy from rising for work. Soon, this morning chatter evolved into meeting for their lunch breaks or even catching up at dinner before returning home to the boarding house, hand in hand.

The vast gap in their ages allowed them to sidestep any potential scandal as nobody saw the two of them together and assumed that any sort of romantic relationship could have been going on. An intergenerational friendship, perhaps, but the idea that anything untoward might have been happening seemed almost laughable.

It seems that the two of them were quite aware of how preposterous their relationship appeared on paper because a few short weeks after they met when they went to the church and asked to be wed, they lied on their marriage certificate.

George marked himself down as only 48, while Amelia made herself 30. Still a very sizeable difference in age, but not completely outside of the realm of possibility, particularly at a time when older, wealthier men often wed the young and attractive women who were willing to suffer through their affections for the financial stability that they provided.

Doubtless, there are some who looked upon the marriage between George and Amelia as an arrangement like that, where she was taking advantage of the older man who was so desperate for company and attention that he would take whatever he could get. But whatever gains she made were not financial, George was not a particularly wealthy man although by combining their finances they were able to achieve a better quality of life than either of them could manage alone. If nothing else, marriage provided them both with a financial gain in that they were able to rent one room for married couples instead of two rooms for individuals.

All evidence seems to point toward the two of them actually being a love match, two people together because they enjoyed one another's company, rather than anything more insidious. Amelia had remained a romantic despite everything, so it should come as no surprise the minor matters of practicality like the gap in their age and the limited luxury that George could provide her, did not feature into her decision-making.

Yet to say that she did not benefit from the arrangement would be fundamentally false. Not only was she quite happily married in the sense of enjoying her husband's company and loving him, but also, he provided her with a degree of stability that she had been lacking throughout her time in Bristol. And with that stability came an opportunity for advancement.

As well-educated as Amelia had made herself, it mattered little in the practical world of Bristol. Simply being able to read and write were not remarkable feats there and being well-versed in poetry and the classics did not actually translate into her being any more employable. But now with George able to financially support the pair of them, she was able to get out of the grind of barely scraping by and having no time to improve herself and her situation.

With her background in Greek, Latin, and the fundamentals of science learned from her father's books, Amelia was an ideal candidate for medical training. And while the idea of a female doctor was still a flight of fancy in 1861, there was no question that she could train as a nurse.

With her life experience, it should come as no surprise that Amelia excelled as a nurse-in-training. She impressed everyone that she was sent to work with during her apprenticeship years and offered a degree of caring and compassion that her patients often described as "maternal". Despite this record of excellence, though, there was something about the job that sat wrong with Amelia. Self-reflection had never been one of her strongest suits. Even so, one might have expected a girl, traumatised in her youth by being forced into the role of a caretaker, to avoid seeking out such a career as an adult. Amelia had failed to make this connection and drudged on with a sense of despondency constantly hovering over her. So much of her life had been spent in misery and unhappiness that now when she should have been able to experience joy and contentment, she could feel no difference. There can be no question that George Thomas was the love of her life, nor that the life that they had built together was the happiest she had ever been, but it was inexorably counterbalanced by her inherent sense of anguish and inescapable melancholy.

During the course of her nursing duties, Amelia crossed paths with a midwife by the name of Ellen Dane who was favorably impressed with Amelia's work. As it turns out, Ellen

46

operated a side business that, in a way, complemented her usual duties. Life was exceedingly difficult for unwed mothers during the Victorian period. Laws had been passed removing all financial obligation from the fathers of illegitimate children which resulted in the women being unfairly penalised by burdening them with the wholly untenable reality of being solely responsible for supporting themselves and their children. Since they were essentially shunned and rejected by society at large, they were effectively rendered incapable of finding respectable work or any viable means of income to meet their basic needs. Historically, the wealthy upper echelons had always relied upon extended family in the countryside to adopt and raise those babies illegitimately conceived by their own daughters, but the less fortunate women had no such safety net. Consequently, a burgeoning submarket soon flourished in the cities, ushered in by the Industrial Revolution. Just because a thing was stigmatised and made borderline illegal did not mean that human nature was changed. People still found love outside the bonds of marriage and that love inevitably contributed to the continuation of the human race. All about the cities, homes were transformed into makeshift maternity wards where, for a nominal fee, women could retreat from their daily lives and hide their pregnancy until such time as they came to term and delivered their babies. Some of these establishments were legitimate businesses with ties to actual adoption agencies or to the church. They would accept the mothers' charitable donations and use the funds to find permanent homes for the abandoned babies. Far more common than these well-meaning businesses, tragically, was a new trend that became known as "baby farming". It was this business model that Ellen Dane had taken up, serving first as a midwife in the baby farms of others, and then moving on to operate her own farm out of a converted townhouse in suburbia.

In these less legitimate baby farms, the goal was not to seek adoption for the children. Such a process would have been lengthy and involved, not to mention entirely in opposition to the principles of making as much money as quickly as possible before closing the operation down and moving on to avoid the attention of the authorities. Instead, unscrupulous farmers would starve the newborns with the intent of cutting costs and hastening the demise of the children so that their cots could be filled by another paying customer. Queen Victoria's privy council became involved in the investigation of this practice because it was so widespread and it was Dr Greenhow, the royal family's personal physician, who is credited with discovering the means by which so many young children could be kept undetected in urban areas.

Godfrey's Cordial, often known as 'Mother's Friend', was an over-the-counter medicine sold freely to the mothers of young children as a cure for colic and poor sleep. While many of the ingredients were entirely harmless to the babies, the active ingredients in the syrup were opiates. Although there were many similar preparations widely available, most relied on the sedative effects of alcohol, instead. Dr Greenhow discovered that the preference for Godfrey's Cordial among baby farmers was not simply a matter of easy access, but that it was deliberately sought after as a sedative because of a well-known side effect of opium abuse: the loss of appetite. Children could be starved to death silently without any demanding agonized wailing, lost in an opiate haze from the moment they were born to the moment that they passed.

As such, there was no need for deliberate acts of murder, and any babies examined by the coroner would be found to have simply died from malnutrition. Their cause of death was listed as 'debility from birth' or simply 'starvation.' The only ones liable to check up on these children after they had been handed off to the baby farmers were their mothers and families, families that had deliberately sent these children away because they did not want them. It was a rare woman indeed who would go back to check up on her 'nurse child' and rarer still were those who would attempt to push through the barriers that were raised against them.

The farmers would insist that it was bad for the child to meet its mother, that it would confuse the child and make it more difficult to find them an adoptive home. It was better to make a clean cut, severing the old life from the new and guaranteeing a better future for the baby. If this was unsuccessful, they would spin tales of homes in the countryside where those children who were found to be sickly were transferred so that they might enjoy fresher air. Addresses were given out that led nowhere by the people operating the farms. They felt safe in the knowledge that few if any of the impoverished women that they had taken children from would ever be able to raise enough funds to leave the city and seek out the places to which they were directed.

Even when suspicions were raised, the families of the missing children had no real legal recourse. The entire business operated in a very murky grey area on the periphery of the law and there was no telling who would suffer the consequences if these matters were brought to the police. More pressingly for many of these families, there would have been the issue of scandal to contend with. If they made a fuss, then it was quite possible that their secret would come out. Surely, it was better to just take the baby farmers at face value rather than risk dragging their names through the dirt.

To make matters worse, on those rare occasions when the authorities did investigate, they would find nothing. Every one of these baby farms was a temporary setup ready to move on as soon as a full crop of babies had been collected and disposed of, often within a matter of weeks. At best, the police would find only remnants of the farm, cots too broken to be carried off to the next location or a few tattered and stained blankets. Perhaps there had been a report from the neighbours that they had suspected something was amiss, but never anything more substantial. The baby farmers were organised, and they were smart about their campaign of evil. More importantly, from a societal level, they were acceptable. They were doing what society, on some level, wanted done. Nobody would admit out loud that they wanted all the illegitimate babies in the world to die, but there were few who would not concede that it was a tidy solution to the moral iniquities of the lower classes, who bred like rabbits anyway.

This constant flight from the authorities meant that Ellen and Amelia only had a short time together before the midwife eventually fled by boat to the United States to avoid police attention. In their brief time together, though, Amelia had learned more than enough about the operation of these baby farms, enough that she could easily operate one of her own with very little effort.

She began to consider this new occupation while still working as a nurse, but circumstances saw to it that her working days would soon be cut short as she fell pregnant with a child of her own. Ellen Dane may have only been a brief visitor in Amelia's life, but it seems that she left a deep impression given that when her own baby girl was born, Amelia chose to name it Ellen.

Without the constant miseries of reliving her worst traumas working as a nurse, this truly became the happiest time in Amelia's life. She had a husband that she loved, a home of her own, and a daughter that she doted on. All of the things that she had been told were the hallmarks of a happy life now belonged to her and, finally, she began to let go of the memories that had haunted her. At least until she was forced to relive them all over again.

With a thirty-five-year gap between their ages, George Thomas had been significantly older than Amelia when they first met and now, eight years later, the gap in their ages became ever more apparent as he became bedridden. For the second time in her life, Amelia had to serve as both housewife and carer. But while she had watched her mother die slowly of her sickness with a mounting sense of relief that she would soon be freed from her duties, she now had to watch the slow, inexorable decline of the man that she loved. She had borne witness to the horrors of watching the ravages of illness drain the vitality and life from someone before, but now she was also burdened with a terrible practicality. She was reliant upon George's income to keep a roof over her and her daughter's heads. His death would not simply be a matter of sadness but of survival. It would almost have been kinder if his death had been abrupt. At least then the drain upon their finances would have been instantaneous rather than relentless and protracted. As it was, they drew closer to poverty with every passing day. They received no income from George's work as he could no longer work, and all of the costs of living seemed amplified as their meagre savings steadily dwindled.

When George Thomas finally died in 1869, Amelia was as close to broke as she had ever been. The little nest egg that they'd set aside from their shared wages, and the payoff she had received from her family had been consumed by long months of nobody working, a sickly husband and a small child draining the coffers.

Now more than ever, she was in desperate need of a quick injection of cash and it seemed that the career path that Ellen Dane had laid out for her was the most viable option.

Once more she failed to consider the devastating psychological effects that her choices would inflict upon her. When she'd been contemplating this course before it had been as a married woman, but not as a mother. Now she would have to contend with the discordant emotions wrought from raising her own daughter with all the love and affection that she intended while willfully neglecting and essentially killing other children. Children who looked barely perceptibly different from her own child. This, much like choosing her career in nursing, should have taken a terrible toll on Amelia, but at this point, she was so numb to horror that it was difficult to say whether she was even aware of the harm that she was doing herself.

She advertised her services as a trained nurse alongside assurances that she was a respectable married woman who could provide a loving home for any child regardless of the circumstances of its birth. From the very moment that she placed her advertisement in the paper, she was committed to this course. She was ready to kill the most innocent in society to put bread upon her own table.

She was ready to look down into the eyes of her daughter and smile as the cold still bodies of tiny babies lay rotting in another room of their home, so doused in opium that it could still be smelt off them as they decomposed.

Bristol and Bedlam

Making a career as a baby farmer was almost painfully easy, people were willing to believe anything if it aligned with their interests, and it was quite firmly in the interest of everyone involved for the babies placed into Amelia's care to vanish as promptly as possible. Yet the quality of clients that she was receiving tended towards the lower end of the socio-economic classes. They were desperate women with absolutely nothing to their names who could only pay in the region of £5 at most to have their little problem taken care of. Amelia was well aware that if a baby had parents who were well-off they could possibly command a fee as high as £80. Even those middling-value children born of fathers who did not wish to deal with embarrassment - typically married men who had strayed - would secure at least £50. Amelia wanted to climb that ladder, she wanted to see a better return on the investment of her time and efforts. Such aspirations may come with additional risks in the form of better-connected victims, but she had all of her friend Ellen's tricks of the trade to fall back on if anyone ever did come looking for a baby that no longer existed. In order to achieve her goal of upgrading her clientele, she was going to have to begin projecting an appearance of respectability that, at present, she was not capable of. Her current clients were providing enough income to keep a roof over her head and food in her belly, but they certainly were not lifting her up out of poverty at a rate of only £5 per baby.

Amelia could still remember what it was like when she had first married George Thomas and how all of her problems had simply melted away. From there, it did not take her long to come to the conclusion that another husband might provide exactly what she needed. A proper marriage would not only provide the financial gains to get her out of shabby old clothes and dingy dwellings, but it would also provide the appearance of respectable stability as a real mother with a real family behind her. It would provide her with the image of all the things she often had to assure her clients she could offer when convincing them to part with their babies.

For three years she had managed alone, but every day had felt like a struggle. She was still weighed down by grief over the loss of her beloved husband, even if she did not recognize her current state of misery as coming from anything other than her material circumstances. She very likely assumed that her grief and loneliness would evaporate along with her financial woes with the acquisition of another man to fill that emptiness in her life.

So it came to pass that she did exactly the thing that she'd sworn she would never do, exactly the thing that had driven her to choose to burn all bridges with her family by pursuing a sufficient inheritance to circumvent any need for a husband. She went out deliberately looking for a man to be a father to her daughter and a breadwinner for their household.

What she found in 1872 was a man by the name of William Dyer. William was a functional alcoholic who had always struggled to hold down work or a relationship as a result of his addiction. He bounced from one-day labour job to another over the years until finally settling in Bristol where he worked at a brewery, staying close to his one true love even while he could not actively consume it. This was not the love match that Amelia had with her first husband, it barely qualified as a courtship at all. The romance that Amelia had so desperately craved all her life after having her dreams infused with it by the literature she read was nowhere to be found. Their pairing was a rough and carnal affair that the rather dim William probably didn't even realise was the prelude to marriage. Had he been entirely sober, he likely would never have found his way to the altar. The countless personality clashes between the newlyweds gave rise to blazing rows that went on for weeks or months at a time. Most of the arguments were primarily spawned from disagreements over the management of their shared finances. The fact that Amelia had her own business that she operated had seemed like a boon to William in the beginning. He had imagined it would provide him with ample drinking money, but it soon became apparent that Amelia had no intention of parting with a single penny that she herself had earned and, instead, intended to use William's rather meagre income to supplement her own in her pursuit of upward social mobility. To William, this seemed like a complete waste of effort and cash. Other men might have sought to improve themselves but William was content to wallow in the life that he'd been born into. To him, extra money meant less time sober, not nicer clothing or fresh whitewash for the walls. There was no equality in their relationship. While William may have expected to be the authority figure, given the power disparity between men and women in Victorian society, it had probably never occurred to him that his domineering new wife would be the one wearing the trousers in their relationship and, more importantly, holding the purse strings tight.

Despite their ceaseless bickering and vast disagreements over the direction that their life should take, it seemed that their relationship was not entirely without love, at least of the physical sort, given that they had two children together. A girl named Mary Ann, who went through life known to everyone as Polly, and a little boy that they named William Samuel.

The lacklustre marriage continued for half a decade of perpetual fighting and bouts of drunken violence before Amelia finally decided that it would be easier to simply pretend with her clients to have a husband who was always busy with work rather than trying to pass William off for a decent man as he lounged around the house drunk.

Divorce was practically unheard of in Victorian Society, especially among the lower classes who were, ironically, more socially conservative than the aristocrats handing down the laws from on high. Even so, eventually, William's abuse and general uselessness outweighed any social stigma that might be attached to Amelia. It would be far easier to play the widow and act as though all three children were born of the same father rather than dealing with another moment of William's antics.

It was at about this point in Amelia's baby farming career that she decided to forgo the inconvenience and expense of actually caring for the children that had been placed under her watch. There had been a great many accidental deaths up until this point, and no shortage of opium-induced starvation, but for the most part, Amelia had at least tried to keep the babies alive. This effort was now abandoned. Her goal became to eliminate the children as swiftly as possible with the minimum amount of fuss as, at some point after her own children had come of age, she entirely lost any desire to perform actual childcare.

It was during this period that Amelia first came to the attention of the police. Law enforcement was, at the time, ostensibly cracking down on baby farms. As a smoke screen, Amelia would take long breaks from her career as a foster mother and return to nursing. Ironically, given her childhood, the area of nursing where she found the most success was actually in asylums caring for the mentally ill. Her many years of experience dealing with her mother had left her uniquely well-equipped to talk down the emotionally unstable and when that empathy failed her, she was also uniquely willing to resort to violence to control her wards. Most nurses would excel in either one or the other depending upon their temperament, but in Amelia there was a nurse who could go to either extreme, treating the deranged with an uncommon kindness when it served her purposes or manhandling them like slabs of meat when they were disobedient.

Switching back and forth from legitimate work as a nurse and the legal grey area of baby farming as needed when it became expedient to avoid detection and trouble, she made it until 1879 before serious suspicions about her began to be raised.

A doctor, troubled by the number of child deaths he'd been called on to certify at Amelia's property, filed a report with the police suggesting that they investigate the premises on the off-chance that there was anything untoward happening.

When the police arrived to investigate, they found all the hallmarks of a baby farm from the rows of cots, barely used, to the copious amounts of opiates ready to ply the babies with. What they did not find were any dead children, only a few newborns who seemed none the worse for wear. The history of the place coupled with the sheer number of death certificates that had been issued for infants in Amelia's care were sufficient to have it shut down, and in all likelihood, she could easily have been convicted of murder or manslaughter at this point. However, neither of these charges were pursued by the courts even though it would have been a simple matter to make them stick. Instead, the judge decided to charge Amelia only with neglect and hand down the incredibly lenient sentence of six months of hard labour. This was during a time when you could face multiple years behind bars for stealing a loaf of bread. Why the judge elected to give such a gentle tap on the wrist to Amelia was not entirely clear. Maybe he took pity on her as a widow and a mother of children of her own. Maybe he did not believe that she had been deliberately doing harm to the children in her care. Or maybe he simply believed that she was providing a valuable service by purging the lower classes of the next generation.

Regardless, despite how lenient the sentence was, it was apparently sufficient to do untold damage to Amelia. She would later be described as having undergone a complete nervous breakdown as a result of her imprisonment, never fully recovering from the experience of being jailed. Despite everything that she endured up until this point in her life, Amelia had nonetheless remained mentally stable. Her actions had sometimes been driven by emotion rather than logic, but they had never been erratic or ill-conceived. This would now change as the careful and calculating woman who had taken such great care to avoid detection and maintain an air of respectability was dead, she'd died in a Bristol prison cell and all that was left behind was her body still going through the motions and plans that had already been laid out for it.

Upon release from jail, she decided to focus on a legitimate career as a nurse, feeling quite certain that she was not cut out for criminality given that the relatively mild punishment that she had already received had been more than sufficient to break her. She returned to working in bedlam houses and mental wards but now found she had more in common with the patients than she did her coworkers. The nervous tremors that afflicted them could be seen in her own hands. The eyes darting from one corner of a room to another searching for danger, were her own eyes. Paranoia, depression, and thoughts of suicide had seen many of the patients in her care committed, and now here she was walking among them in her pristine white uniform feeling exactly as they felt.

Her financial situation had not improved as a result of abandoning the more lucrative of her two pursuits, and while her children were now old enough to go out into the world and take responsibility for their own incomes, little of it flowed back to the matriarch of the Dyer clan. She was loved and respected by her children as much as anyone who had done the things that she had done could expect to be loved and respected, but none of them were so well-off or well-established that she could expect to retire in comfort under their watchful eyes. So she was faced with the dilemma, to pursue her illegal enterprise once more or allow herself to slip back into the dark depths of poverty.

After the crisis of imprisonment, Amelia had begun to find hardship in the grind of her everyday life. All the little things that never used to get to her now seemed insurmountable obstacles and all of the little sorrows that she thought she'd set behind her now loomed large in her mind. Where before, the threat of poverty had seemed an abstract and fearful thing, she now began to see it as an inevitable reality, creeping up on her with the same inescapable certainty as death. And confronted with the possibility of having to live in a poor house or commit herself to work in one of the many 'charitable' ventures that the industrialists of the time had set up to keep the idle hands of the underclass occupied, she never found the horror to be too much to contemplate. She was quite willing to do anything to avoid it, even if it did run the risk of another brush with the law.

Her time in prison had given her plenty of time to contemplate where she had gone wrong in her last criminal enterprise, and she believed that she had spotted the weak point in the web of deception that she wove. It was the involvement of the doctor signing death certificates for the babies that had resulted in her prosecution so she would simply remove the doctor from the equation. No longer would those that died in her care receive a good Christian burial at a Potter's Field, instead she would deal with the gruesome remains of the dead herself. In days past, Amelia would have quickly recognized the additional risks involved in disposing of the children's bodies for herself. She would have understood the greatly increased chances of discovery that came in the absence of some legal mechanism rendering the children in her care officially gone, not to mention the risk involved should she be seen transporting or destroying human remains. All these dangers would have been readily recognized and weighed into her decision-making process. In days past, she could have probably devised some clever means of avoiding the pitfalls of these additional risks, but at this point, all rationality had been lost as a result of her nervous breakdown. She was now governed more by her base fears than by any sort of reason or logic.

As fate would have it, it was actually this instability that was the source of her problems more than her illegal baby farming operation, as she soon caught the attention of the mental health professionals that surrounded her on a daily basis.

Over the course of several years, Amelia's business waxed and waned as her ability to pass herself off as a respectable member of society faltered and her client base began to dry up. Making her financial situation worse was the fact that she had begun self-medicating, using alcohol and opium products like she had been using to quiet the babies. A little spoonful for them, a little spoonful for her to make the miserable days feel a little less miserable. While some pointed to this substance abuse as the source of her ever-increasing instability, it seems more likely to have been a case of correlation rather than causation; the worse her mental state, the more she would self-medicate, the more she would self-medicate, the clumsier her actions would become and the more consequences she would have to face as a result. Obviously, this could lead nowhere but to a downward spiral.

Of course, nothing could be so damaging a trigger to her mental instability as the threat of another imprisonment. As such, each time that she caught wind of a police investigation into her operations she began to abuse her medications of choice even more heavily which resulted in ever-greater lapses in judgement. Ultimately, her behaviour could no longer go unnoticed. Eventually, the police showed up for a visit to the townhouse to investigate allegations of a baby farm being run there only to discover that the place had been abandoned following the tenant being committed to a bedlam house.

This first spell in a mental hospital actually proved to be of great benefit to Amelia, not only because it allowed her to lay low while police interest died down, but also because it offered her a degree of stability that she had not been capable of creating for herself. Her meals were provided at a fixed time every day, she was guaranteed a bed every night, and all of the pressures that suffocated her in her day-to-day life, ranging from trying to secure shifts for her legitimate work to trying to secure clients for her illegitimate work, were eliminated. All that she had to do while she was in Bedlam was exist, behave herself and cause no trouble. She had a great deal of experience working in institutions of this sort, so she knew exactly what she needed to do to keep the staff happy and ensure that she would soon receive a clean bill of mental health.

Upon her release, she returned to her life invigorated and refreshed and treated the whole thing as though it had been a holiday. Marshalling her newly rejuvenated spirits, she was determined to make a fresh start for herself. Returning to work in mental hospitals after having just been released from one as a patient seemed ill-conceived, but she was convinced that her extensive experience in childcare made her an ideal fit for the role of governess. If only she could just pass for someone with just a little more refinement and class, she could have secured for herself a well-paying job with room and board in one of the wealthier homes in the city. She could not do so. Instead, Amelia found a sub-market to occupy, serving as a child-minder for those women who were governesses so that they could abandon their duties and go off to enjoy their substantial pay instead of being encumbered with a baby all day.

Compared to what the governesses were paid, Amelia was making but a pittance but it was still drastically more than she had to be able to command as a nurse. In fact, it almost matched the income that she was able to secure at the height of her baby farming days. Old habits die hard, however. And she soon began dosing her wards with laudanum, a derivative of opium that saw much use at the time as a painkiller and nerve tonic. Laudanum that she herself was abusing almost every day.

In 1890, one of the governesses that had been providing her with steady work came to Amelia with a little problem of her own, a pregnancy that had resulted from a dalliance with the master of the house. She did not dare raise the matter with her employer because even if she were able to convince him to part with some money, it would nonetheless be the end of her career and the destruction of her reputation. She needed the baby in her belly to not exist, for it to entirely vanish from sight the very moment that it was out of her so that she could return to her duties caring for its legitimate half-siblings.

Amelia was only too happy to oblige, as this governess represented a distinct improvement over her typical baby farming client base. A classier kind of client that would bring with it significantly higher upfront payments.

What she failed to account for was her ongoing business relationship with this governess and the fact that she would continue to see her with regularity. As much as the governess may have wanted the baby to disappear from the sight of society, that did not mean that she did not still care for her child. Indeed, if she had intended to be rid of the little boy permanently, then it would have been a rather foolish move to place him in the care of someone that she saw so frequently.

After a few short weeks parted from her child, the governess returned to check up on him and was shocked to discover that the baby presented to her seemed to bear no relation to the one that she had left behind. At that moment it was her word against Amelia's that they were looking at the same baby as had been left in her care, but there was a very simple way to establish the truth of the matter. Unbeknownst to Amelia, who had barely given the child a second look before disposing of it, the governess's son had a distinctive birthmark on one of his hips. Stripping the baby down revealed no such mark, only unblemished skin.

Throwing caution and all thoughts of her career and reputation to the wind, the governess went immediately to the police to report what had happened and they soon arrived to question Amelia. The woman that they met could not have been more different from the shrewd and calculating manipulator that the last policemen to cross her path had encountered. She was visibly upset to the point of quaking and weeping over the accusation that had been levelled against her, and utterly distraught at the idea that she might have done any baby harm.

There were obviously a great many downsides to Amelia's mental instability, but there could be no denying that her erratic emotional responses made for a very convincing liar. As questioning went on, her mental state seemed to deteriorate further and she grew more and more upset, eventually snatching up two full bottles of laudanum from her desk and drinking them down in an attempted suicide right before the officers' eyes.

Everything about the missing baby was immediately forgotten as the crisis unfolded. Typically, a dose of laudanum was drawn from the bottle in a pipette, one tiny droplet at a time. The amount of distilled opiate that she consumed in that moment should have been sufficient to kill not only her but a full-grown ox.

She was rushed to the hospital by the police officers and the doctors did everything in their power to save the woman but having heard just how hefty a dose that she had taken, the general consensus was that their efforts were doomed to failure. Nobody could consume that much laudanum and survive.

Not unless they had spent years abusing opiates to the point that they had developed a remarkably high tolerance to them.

Amelia Dyer survived her suicide attempt, and the matter of the missing baby was entirely forgotten as she underwent treatment and was eventually discharged into a bedlam house where she might be watched over to ensure that the same thing could not happen again.

There are some who believe that Amelia knew about her resistance to opium and staged the entire thing as a grand manipulation to get out of trouble. However, it seems more likely, given how little was known about the development of opium tolerance at the time, that this was in fact a legitimate suicide attempt to avoid another bout of imprisonment given that her first prison term was what caused the nervous breakdown that led to this point.

After suffering so public a breakdown it became impossible for Amelia to return to her child-minding duties for the various governesses of the city, even if they hadn't believed the rumours circulating that she had tried to pass off someone else's baby as one that had been left in her care. With that avenue entirely closed to her along with her nursing career now at a complete standstill, there was only one thing left for Amelia to do to ensure that she stayed out of the workhouse. She returned to baby farming with renewed gusto and a revised strategy. Completely abandoning any pretence of actually caring for the children, Amelia would only wait barely long enough to be out of sight of the parents before disposing of the infants. Now that starvation was no longer on the table due to the considerable time it took to take effect, her new preferred method of dispatch was strangulation. She would take a length of string, a ribbon or something similar, tie it around the baby's neck and then tighten it until the baby was dead.

The woman who had begun her baby farming career so long ago could not have done this, but the Amelia of 1891 was a different creature entirely. All of the kindness and romance that had once been within her had been burned out by the passage of time and the weight of countless miseries. All that remained was the cold calculating killer that she had become.

Change became the only constant in Amelia's life, and in the life of her children, as they drifted from town to town, constantly changing their names and identities to avoid detection by the authorities who now knew to keep an eye on Mother Dyer. Aliases began to blend together. The different stories that she told as different people became interchangeable. This made matters a lot simpler for Amelia because although she may have been faking some degree of her mental breakdowns to avoid punishment, there could be no denying her mental faculties were degenerating as a result of her ongoing opiate and alcohol abuse, not to mention the unravelling of her personality as she underwent crisis after crisis. If all of her various characters shared some elements in their stories, she did not need to remember any of the things that distinguished them from one another.

Yet despite all the distress the many crises in her life caused her, she always seemed to be driving onward towards the next one as though she took some sick pleasure in it.

In a perversely obscure way, it was affirming to her nihilist outlook on life to be confronted with constant problems as it provided her with the moral justification that she needed to 'survive' these situations. It granted a free license to do as she pleased regardless of the consequences for others. If the world was an evil and hostile place, then everything that she did was justified and those who did not pursue the easiest, albeit least ethical, course were fools and in complete denial about the nature of reality. With such a worldview, Amelia could justify anything no matter how wicked or wretched.

Amidst all of the many aliases that she went under, her children struggled to recall the name that they were supposed to be calling her by, so it was that she assumed the ultimate blank canvas alias that could be applied to her in any situation. From that point on, nobody was to call her by her name and she would not even put her own name to paper in case she made a mistake and scribbled down the wrong alias. Her children were to call her "mother". Their various partners were to call her "mother". Even the clients that she met with and convinced to part with their newborn children found themselves defaulting to that title.

It isn't clear whether she appreciated the irony of titling herself "mother", while committing an ongoing slaughter of innocent babies or if her faculties were too far gone by this point to even recognise how grotesque it was.

Bouncing from place to place, never putting down roots and never establishing connections, it became impossible for Amelia to find the kind of security that she craved. Her very worst fears came to pass in many of the cities where she found herself. The workhouses where the impoverished were essentially enslaved until they could clear their debts, the very places that she had most feared being committed to became a regular feature of her life. She spent months at a time between her baby farm projects, and the income that came along with them, labouring alongside the most desperate and destitute in society.

During this period of time, she was forced to confront degrees of stress and unhappiness that she had never expected to become a part of her life.

Not surprisingly, her mental health continued to suffer.

There is certainly an argument to be made that each time one of her aliases was gaining too much attention, Amelia would have another very public breakdown and allow herself to be confined to a bedlam house as a tactical move. But it also seems reasonable that these nervous breakdowns were the result of the immense pressures that she was constantly putting herself under, rather than being deliberate obfuscations that she was using to avoid detection. Logical and cogent arguments have been presented for both theories, that her breakdowns were being faked and that her breakdowns were genuine. Given that she had a generally pleasant time while incarcerated in mental hospitals in comparison to her day-to-day life, it is unsurprising that many people believe she was choosing to be there rather than enduring her far more difficult life on the outside.

There may have been an element of this at play, but it is impossible to look at her behaviour during these breakdowns and see any way in which they might have benefited her. A more likely scenario is that she genuinely suffered mental health crises, was incarcerated as a result, and then came to her senses once in custody allowing her to manipulate her way out again.

This would all change in 1893 when Amelia was committed to the Somerset and Bath Pauper's Lunatic Asylum near the town of Wells. This was not one of the comfortable hospitals in which she had served out her previous periods of convalescence, nor one of the pleasant places that she had worked when she served as a nurse. It was for all intents and purposes a dumping ground for all of society's most unwanted. The mentally disabled, the profoundly mentally ill, and even in some cases, just the exceptionally poor or those whose minds had broken under the strain of living their terrible lives.

It was a cramped and dirty place where the patients were crammed into rooms so full that they could not have laid down on the cold ground even if they had wanted to because there were simply too many bodies in the way. Treatment, such as it was, consisted of a series of minor tortures inflicted on the patients with the vague hope of shocking them out of their madness. Treatment modalities included such things as hydrotherapy with chilled water, long periods of being suspended upside down to increase blood flow to the brain and any number of other things that the predominantly untrained and uneducated staff chose to inflict upon them. Psychiatric treatment may have been in its very early infancy during this time period, but almost nothing prescribed by the 'doctors' of the Pauper's Lunatic Asylum was ever codified as a genuinely useful type of therapy in the years to come. Rather, the treatment of the mad was more reminiscent of medieval times when it was thought that madness or wickedness could be eradicated from the body through the judicious application of sufficient physical pain.

Amelia had suffered in her life, this much was undeniable, and one could even say that her suffering had defined her and transformed her into the person that she was as an adult, but beyond the occasional backhanded slap from her second husband, when during their frequent arguments, her words cut too deep for him to scrounge up a rebuttal, the physical aspect of her suffering had been relatively limited. She had known hunger, and the pain of backbreaking labour in the workhouse, but actual torture had been unknown to her until that moment. She would become intimately familiar with it in the weeks and months to follow her arrival in Somerset and Bath Asylum, enduring every torment and humiliation that the staff could concoct to amuse themselves. Unfortunately for Amelia, tricking her way out was nowhere near as simple as it had been on previous occasions, either. It was almost as though the staff didn't actually care if she was cured of her melancholy or not. As though they actually had no intention of helping their patients, hurting them not for their own good, or for any holy mechanism which might flagellate away their sins, but simply because they wanted to hurt someone.

Their desire to inflict pain for no reason other than their own twisted entertainment made no sense to Amelia. When she caused someone else pain, it was always with a purpose. It was always to alleviate her own suffering or to further her agenda. Causing harm for no discernible purpose was offensive to her personal morals, such as they were, and so she would respond to her own torment and the torment of others with aggressive outbursts that often saw her confined with black marks set against her name marking her as a disruptive element. Prison and bedlam had both been easy for her to navigate before because she had never been forced to contend with an entirely broken system that punished the innocent and gave total power to the vicious. Her current reality was far too similar to the outside world for her liking. Too arbitrary and cruel. She wanted out as soon as she arrived, but because of how arbitrary and cruel the system was; she was trapped.

For months on end, she was held in the pauper's bedlam, desperate to escape but clashing constantly with those in charge because all her attempts at manipulation ultimately failed. They didn't want anything from her, she had nothing to give them, ergo, she would go on suffering until they got bored of her, or until it benefitted them to let her go, and not a moment sooner.

It was stress that had always driven Amelia to the point of her nervous breakdowns, which in turn resulted in long periods confined to mental hospitals where she slowly recovered from the experience. This time, however, the source of her stress was the mental hospital itself, and there was no escaping from it until she could show that she no longer needed to be there. The catch was, of course, that the longer she was in the hospital, the worse her condition became resulting in more and more crises for her to contend with. Each time she suffered another nervous breakdown while in the tender care of the bedlam house, her torments would be amplified in double measure with the alleged intent of curing her, this would drive her on to further breakdowns and further punishment, creating an infinite loop from which she could never fully recover enough to regain any control of her situation. She had been a stout and robust woman when they had taken her into custody, but it would take almost two years after her release for her to fully recover and regain all the weight she had lost during her confinement. Even then, there were marks from the torments she endured that would never fully fade. She would still flinch at any loud noise; her hands would quake and tremor at unexpected moments. The time that she had spent in the asylum had changed her, but exclusively for the worse. None of the genuine mental illness that plagued her was ever addressed, and her treatment at the hands of the staff only served to exacerbate many of her issues, not to mention proving to her once and for all that the world was a hostile place where only those willing to do evil could survive and thrive.

She would not talk about her time in the asylum after her release, with all that we know about her experiences coming from third parties, but when directly asked about it, she would describe her stay there as a disagreeable experience. And her actions proved more than anything else that she never intended to be put in such a position or such a place again. No matter how dire matters became for her in the years to come, she had closed the door on the escape route that madness provided her. Even when she was in the midst of the worst breakdowns of her life, she would not talk to any doctors, or contemplate putting herself in anyone else's care. Amelia's previous positive experiences with other bedlam houses speak to the potential therapeutic benefit to someone who had been forced to care for a madwoman being offered the same care and kindness, in turn. For Amelia, though, that was no longer an option as she had effectively cut herself off from the possibility on the off chance of a repeat of her dreadful experience with the Somerset and Bath Lunatic Asylum.

Doris Marmon

Following her final period of incarceration, Amelia took some time to recover before setting out to secure a future for herself.

While her children had been content enough to follow after her through her many moves over the years, they were now old enough to have lives of their own, rendering them somewhat useless as props when she was trying to convince others to part from their babies.

During her recovery time, Amelia returned to the workhouse as she was yet incapable of operating businesses as usual. It was a brief stint, but a surprisingly profitable one for Amelia as she used the opportunity to recruit a younger woman from among those forced into labour there to serve as a facsimile daughter when she was attempting to provide the front of a happy family. Jane Smith, known as Granny Smith to her friends, was about the same age as Amelia's daughter Polly and soon fell under the more experienced woman's sway. Granny Smith had nothing and nobody in her life, so the small scraps of affection and attention that Amelia offered her were sufficient to buy her loyalty. Not to mention the fact that through Amelia's intervention, she was able to get herself out of the poor house.

In 1895, when Amelia departed for a fresh start in Caversham, Berkshire, Granny Smith accompanied her with every intention of working for her on the new baby farm she intended to set up. Amelia's daughter Polly and her new husband Arthur Palmer also accompanied the older woman as they had not yet been able to raise the funds to secure a home for themselves. But while Polly and Arthur meant to make a life for themselves, setting out to find work in Caversham, Granny Smith had no such intentions. Amelia meant to keep her on a tight leash until she was entirely certain of her new associate's loyalty. This meant that the only money Smith could have for herself had to come from Amelia's hand. She had to be entirely reliant on Amelia in all things so that going against the woman who now insisted that she call her 'mother,' would seem like the end of her life.

The act of mother and daughter that the two of them performed for clients was successful, so successful in fact Amelia soon had more clients than she knew what to do with. This rapid acquisition of wealth and veritable swarms of young mothers with questions began to draw attention in the Caversham suburb of Reading, and it was only a matter of time before that attention drew the ire of the authorities.

As such, it was less than a year after their arrival in Caversham that Amelia and Granny Smith were ready to move on again. Every time that she had failed, been caught or been chased had taught Amelia valuable lessons. The first and foremost of these lessons was to trust in the niggling voice of anxiety demanding that she flee at the first hint of trouble. There would be no more eking out the last few coins from a place before making her departure, the very second that Amelia suspected someone was on to her, she was out of there.

Polly and her husband were not ready to relocate after so brief a window of time establishing themselves. Both had just found work for the first time in a long time and were no longer reliant upon Amelia for their survival, and as such when it was announced that they were departing Caversham, they parted ways with Amelia instead.

If it were anyone else, then Amelia would have considered this a betrayal. An affirmation that everyone in the world was just out for themselves and that she was completely right and justified to keep Granny Smith on a short leash to ensure that she didn't go roaming off on her own. But it was Polly. Polly had been with her through it all, watching and learning and loving her mother despite everything that she had done and would go on to do. In Polly, she had always seen herself, as the daughter burdened with too much, but who bravely soldiered on. The only one of her children who had stayed as she had suffered through all the indignities and difficulties of her life instead of fleeing to take care of themselves. She could hardly blame Polly for wanting to have a normal life, so she gave the girl her blessing, promised that they would keep in touch, and left her behind. With her fake daughter at her side, instead.

Amelia and Granny Smith moved, alone, to a house at 45 Kensington Road, in Reading. Just a small jaunt away from the last site where they'd performed their monstrous duties, but far enough to disconnect them from the local community and their suspicions. It was here in Reading that Amelia would have the most success in her career, as it was a large enough town to have need of her services, but small enough that none of the other established baby farmers operating in the country had moved in on it yet. Not to mention the transit routes that flowed through the town, allowing Amelia to traverse the length and breadth of England to meet with clients acquired through newspaper advertising. Making matters even better for Amelia, and worse for everyone else, was the fact that the local police had absolutely no experience in dealing with baby farmers or others of that ilk, with the majority of their local women travelling down to London and securing the services of one of the capitol's problem solvers if they found themselves inappropriately pregnant.

So long as Amelia did not get greedy and snatch up a great many babies in the local area as quickly as they had at the last house, they could likely pass entirely undetected for an extended period, meaning no more running.

It was a dream come true for Amelia, an escape from all the troubles that had dogged her footsteps since she first began her criminal career. By the very next morning, she had letters sent off to half a dozen regional newspapers, a few pennies enclosed to pay for the placement of her adverts in the miscellaneous section.

'Married couple with no family would adopt a healthy child, nice country home, terms £10'

It was hardly a generous offer given that Amelia would also demand clothing and toys be provided for the child, all of which would then find their way to the pawn shop providing her with a second stream of income. The ten-pound price point being mentioned up front was primarily an attempt to weed out the poor class of clientele that she had to make do with for so long. £10 was hardly a substantial amount, but it was more than sufficient to eliminate those on the lowest rungs of society for whom holding such a lump sum would be practically impossible. There were many takers of this offer but the one who would gain the most infamy was Evelina Marmon.

Evelina was a barmaid who worked in Cheltenham, popular and pretty at only 25 years old, it came as little surprise to those who worked with her that she became pregnant with an illegitimate child. When questioned she could not name the father, whether out of some sense of obligation to not drag his name through the dirt, or simply because she did not recall it given the number of gentlemen callers she had received through the months of 1895. Such things were, of course, commonplace when it came to bar staff and there were few among her coworkers who had not been in the same situation once or twice throughout their lives. Even the owner was sympathetic, or at least his wife was sympathetic enough for the both of them and had him hen-pecked enough that he would obey her demands to treat the young woman kindly.

She would give birth to her daughter in January 1896 in the boarding house where she lived and promptly began seeking offers of adoption by placing an advertisement in the local paper. By pure coincidence when she picked up a copy of the Bristol Times and Mirror, to check how her posting had been printed, there was Amelia's own advertisement printed right alongside it.

Evelina's intention was to put her daughter Doris into the temporary care of another woman so that she might return to work, build up some savings, and eventually relocate somewhere outside of Cheltenham where the exact circumstances of her daughter's birth would not be common knowledge, and she herself might pass for a widow rather than a harlot. Despite the unfortunate nature of her birth, it seemed that Doris had completely captured the heart of her mother and the two of them had bonded quickly to the degree that even though Evelina was posting advertisements seeking someone to take the baby, it was only with a great deal of trepidation and encouragement from others. If Doris had remained with her mother, then the two of them would most likely have been condemned to poverty as there were not many childcare facilities for the working commoner in Victorian England. She would not have been able to work, or at least not enough to ensure that their boarding house fee was paid off each week, and so they would have ended up homeless or in the poor house. On top of this practical concern, there was the matter of reputation. If it became known that Evelina had a child out of wedlock her reputation would have been in ruins and no respectable establishment would have hired her on, even to serve as a barmaid. The less respectable an establishment was, the lower it would pay its employees and so her slip into poverty was once again assured.

With circumstances forcing her hand, Evelina quickly replied to the advertisement that had been printed alongside hers and a woman by the name of 'Mrs Harding' swiftly answered. The name was one of Amelia's various aliases that she operated under.

From Oxford Road in Reading, the letter that she received from Mrs Harding was essentially a boilerplate letter that Amelia used for all of her fishing expeditions in the papers. She hadn't even been the one to write it, simply giving Granny Smith the original letter to copy out for her, while she settled by the fire with a nice glass of gin.

It contained a variety of platitudes intended to soothe the conscience and worries of any prospective new mother parting from a child for the first time. 'We are plain homely people in fairly good circumstances. I should be glad to have a dear baby girl I could bring up and call my own. I don't want a child for money's sake but for the company and home comfort. I and my husband are dearly fond of children though we have no child of our own. With me, a child will have a good home and a mother's love.'

Evelina Marmon wrote back to her immediately upon receiving her reply to begin negotiating terms. She was willing to pay the £10 specified, along with providing a box of clothes for the baby as requested but would have preferred a different arrangement, whereby she paid a more affordable weekly fee for the care of the daughter she fully intended to reclaim.

Ultimately this would have come to a much greater sum than £10, assuming that the child lived with the Hardings for more than a few months. Yet Mrs Harding would not relent, she absolutely insisted on the lump sum which she claimed would be put towards the decoration of a nursery for the baby and paying for many of the other initial costs one incurred when bringing a new life into the family.

When it seemed this would be a sticking point for the negotiations, Evelina, who was already over a barrel watching her savings dwindle with each passing day, conceded. She would pay the £10 to have her baby taken care of, even if she had to borrow it from less than reputable sources.

With an agreement in principle, arrangements were made for Mrs Harding to travel from Reading and collect the baby.

The woman who came to Evelina's door was far from the warm motherly figure that she'd come to expect from the letters. Amelia Dyer was now advanced in age and rather stocky in appearance with deep-set wrinkles as a result of her ceaseless worrying and nervous temperament. She could not even muster a smile to greet the clearly heartbroken young woman peering out from behind the boarding house door, at best managing to nod severely in greeting instead of offering any niceties.

At first, Evelina was ready to call the whole thing off just at the sight of this rather dour woman, but as Mrs Harding was allowed into the room it was as though a transformation overtook her. The moment that she laid eyes on baby Doris, her whole face lit up. Involuntarily, her hands stretched out towards the little bundle in its basket. She softened, the shoulders that had been drawn up to her ears slumping down, and a sigh escaping her.

Her whole demeanour shifted to kindness in an instant at the sight of the beautiful healthy baby ready to come home with her. She reached out and took Evelina's hand, giving it a squeeze and promising that she was going to take such good care of their baby, she was going to treat little Doris like she was her own.

Given how smitten the woman clearly was with the baby, Evelina decided to push her luck once more, talking about how unsure she was about the whole thing, about how she had never spent a moment apart from little Doris until now. Mrs Harding gave her all the reassurances that anyone might have needed about how the baby was going to be cared for and loved, but what Evelina had actually been aiming for was a change in the terms of their agreement. She still didn't want to make a single upfront payment when weekly payments would have guaranteed that she'd be getting regular updates on little Doris' progress and happiness. Once more, the stern woman who had come to her door seemed to emerge from beneath the mask of sweetness that

Mrs Harding presented. She told the girl that she'd be happy to write letters and keep her informed of how the baby was getting on, but she couldn't be having all the trouble of going back and forth, and the risk of sending money through the mail. She just wanted to focus her time on the baby, not on the business aspect of this whole relationship.

It worked. Despite having all of the leverage in their current situation, with the baby in hand, and Mrs Harding already having invested in the cost of travelling to town to pick her up, Evelina conceded to the old woman's demands and handed over the ten pounds in cash, a little box containing all of Doris' worldly possessions and attempting to hand over the baby itself only to discover at the last moment that she couldn't bring herself to part from her. Even though she knew that this was what was best for both of them, even though she knew this was the only way that she could work towards a future in which they could be together, still she found herself dithering and hesitating.

Back to her kindly demeanour, Mrs Harding took pity on the poor girl and asked her if she might walk them to the train station, as she wasn't sure of the way. It was an obvious lie, but one that Evelina happily latched onto as an excuse to hold her baby just a little bit longer.

Even when Mrs Harding's train arrived at the platform, Evelina couldn't bring herself to part from the baby, so with a roll of her eyes and a little grumble, Mrs Harding bought the other woman a return ticket as far as Gloucester, so that she could spend that last little bit of time with her child. It was a degree of kindness and empathy that was entirely unexpected from Amelia Dyer. The kind of thing that someone with a conscience might have done. In truth, the train ticket was cheap enough when she'd just pocketed ten pounds, plus whatever the baby clothes would get her at the pawn shop, and if this avoided making a big dramatic scene of a mother handing away her daughter to a stranger, then Amelia was willing to pay a little bit to avoid the attention of any witnesses.

Now when the time came for the baby and her mother to part ways, the situation was entirely different. The scene being witnessed was a young woman and her travelling companion parting ways, with the older woman, perhaps her mother, carrying on with the grandchild in tow. Completely unremarkable, but for the tears on Evelina's cheeks and the sobs that racked her as she walked away from her beloved daughter for what would be the last time.

Amelia had told her mark that she was headed straight home to Reading to get the baby settled into her new nursery, but instead, she also switched trains, heading towards London. She intended to do as little of her bloody business as possible in Reading itself, so as to avoid any local attention, and her own beloved daughter Polly had conveniently provided her with a secondary base of operations right in the middle of the capitol.

After they had parted ways, Amelia's daughter had found work as a dressmaker, and her husband as a labourer, with Polly establishing her own little business out of her home at 76 Mayo Road, Willesden. At 23 years old, she was already more in control of her own life than Amelia had ever been. With a brighter future free from the sordid criminal underworld that her mother had raised her in.

Although Polly had no intention of following in her mother's footsteps, that did not mean that she was free from her shadow or influence. When her mother arrived on her doorstep with a baby, there was not a moment of hesitation before she ushered her inside. The bond between them, one of thoroughly ingrained obedience on Polly's part, had never been broken, despite their lives going in separate directions. Polly was still very much her mother's creature even if she had managed to claw her way out of hell and into something resembling a normal life. It did not even occur to her that she could refuse her mother entry, or that she could decline to be a party to yet another murder.

The baby had begun to cry by the time Amelia arrived in Willesden, long past due for a feed and a change. Both of which sounded like too much work to Amelia. Instead, she proceeded into the living room which had been converted into Polly's workspace, found some white edging tape used in dressmaking, and wound it around the baby's neck. Once, and then a second time, before pulling it taut and tying it in a bow.

The band of white edging tape was not tight enough to kill the baby outright. Some small trickle of air could still make it through and the blood supply to the brain was not cut off. The baby would die but not immediately, not even quickly.

Amelia would sit and watch as the tiny newborn Doris flailed and struggled, lacking the strength to even lift herself up to sitting yet, she now had to contend with a struggle for her life.

Polly did not stay to watch. She had seen this gruesome scene far too many times throughout her life. Instead, she went to the kitchen and prepared tea for her mother and herself, as though this were truly a social call and not merely a convenient murder site.

Amelia sat with the baby Doris for almost half an hour as her movements became less and less frantic. As brain damage set in resulting from the strangulation of her air supply, the child's movements became increasingly feeble. By the end, little Doris showed only spasmodic twitches as the last life drained from her. Through it all, not once did Amelia look away. She might have begun down this awful path out of pure practicality, but somewhere between losing her first husband and losing her mind, she had begun to take pleasure in the killing. To find some measure of joy in robbing an innocent baby of its life. She might have justified it to Granny Smith or Polly as keeping watch over the child until its final moment as if she were doing a kindness, but the truth of the matter was that killing had become an end in itself for Amelia Dyer. It was no longer just a necessary step to reach her goals, but a goal of its own.

Later she would confess that she liked to watch the babies struggle and die. And that it was always over too quickly for her tastes. She could quite easily have killed the babies far quicker if she had wanted to, all it would have taken was an extra twist of the cord at the back of their neck, but she wanted to watch them suffer. She wanted to prolong the moment, to eke as much pleasure out of it as she could before being left with a body to deal with.

The killing came easy to her, but the clean-up afterwards was her least favourite job.

Polly returned once she was certain that the deed was done and helped her mother to wrap the dead baby in an oversized napkin and tie it off. From there they moved on to practical matters, sorting through the clothes that had been provided for the baby to find anything worth keeping and setting the rest aside for the pawnbroker. One pair of girls' boots, still far too big for Doris's tiny pink feet, Amelia took with her when she went to visit the landlady for the property, remembering that she had a little girl who would probably treasure such a gift. While she was there, she quite casually paid Polly's rent for the month with a little of the day's takings. Even now with Polly pulling away from her, she would do things like this, provide for her, remind her that without Amelia around her life would become so much harder. Just like everything else that Amelia did, it was a calculated move to maintain just enough loyalty from the women around her to ensure that it was never worthwhile for them to go against her and speak to the police. Some part of her may have been trying to do a kindness for her daughter rather than making such cold-blooded decisions, but if Amelia Dyer were inclined to kindness, then perhaps there would have been more evidence of it in other parts of her life. None of her other children would receive extravagant gifts from her through the years, only the ones who were complicit in her crimes and whose loyalty needed to be carefully maintained. An argument could be made that she was closest with Polly, but the sad fact of the matter was that she only visited with her daughter during her little business trips. From the moment that they parted ways, there had not been a single social call, only more dead babies that she wanted help disposing of.

Amelia would spend the night there with her daughter, greeting her son-in-law when he came in the door and preparing them all a meal. Though how any of them could have stomached eating when there was a dead infant stuffed into a carpet bag in the living room is anyone's guess.

Come morning, Amelia would depart once more from her daughter's home, but only very briefly. Later that same afternoon she would return to Willesden from London proper, having acquired yet another baby in need of a new home and another pocket full of cash.

Harry Simmons was not the same age as Doris Marmon had been, he was a year and a month in age, but despite enjoying a bit of extra time, he was just as tiny, just as defenceless. His mother had been in a situation quite similar to the one Evelina Marmon had been in, differing in only a few of the less important details. And just as Amelia's arrival with little Doris had played out, so did Amelia's arrival with young Harry. It was almost like an eerie episode of déjà vu. Her daughter greeted her at the door and then made herself scarce because she knew exactly what was to follow. Amelia carrying the crying baby through into Polly's workspace to perform her own awful work. Hunting around for a suitable ligature to choke the life from the newborn without killing it too quickly. It was only here that the repetition diverged. There was no more edging tape. She searched through everything in the room, making a mess of all Polly's carefully ordered and organised supplies, but she could not find anything suitable. With little recourse, Amelia went into the carpet bag where the remains of baby Doris had been stashed the preceding day, she undid the kerchief tied around the dead baby and untied the bow that had held the white tape taut around the base of the infant's blood-bloated head. Though Amelia may have expected the head to deflate like a balloon when the tape was removed, no change in the appearance of little Doris was apparent. There was little time to linger on the dead though, not when the living still needed her immediate attention.

Just as before, she looped the tape twice around the baby's neck, and just as before, she pulled it tight until the screams and cries became muffled, slowly fading away to nothing at all. Again, she sat and watched the entire grim process from start to finish, barely even blinking so that she wouldn't miss a single moment of it.

As humans, we have an innate instinct to protect the young. An innate sense that anything bad happening to someone is infinitely worse if they are under a certain age. It is as close as we come to a hardwired moral directive in the complex mix of sentience and animal instinct influences that we call our minds. As such, it is hard to conceive of anything more evil than slowly strangling a newborn child to death for profit and pleasure, but sitting there and watching the baby die when all that you would have to do is loosen the tape would definitely be one of those things. Killing a baby, we can almost contend with, even torturing a baby, we could understand if there was some terrible sickness that had taken root in the mind of the perpetrator driving them to do unnatural and inhuman things. But what Amelia did, sitting back passively and watching a baby die in the most horrible way, coldly looking on as it was desperately gasping for air with its throat locked almost entirely shut is surely an act of callousness that defies the limits of human imagination to understand how a person could do such a thing.

Regardless of where she had started out, or the discomfort she had suffered as a result of her circumstances, there was nothing that had happened in Amelia's life that could possibly justify what she was doing now. Even the absolute worst of the other baby farmers simply overdosed the children on opiates to make them die on their own. Even the most hardened of criminals could not conceive of killing a baby by hand instead of by neglect, and even among those few truly monstrous individuals who could countenance doing what Amelia did, not one of them would have sat there and watched it happen with an expression of grim delight on her face.

It was evil, pure and simple. She had gone from using the hardships of her life to justify breaking rules to diving so far off the deep end that she could no longer see the sun. There could be no justification for her actions. No explanation that might satisfy those who would demand answers for such awful acts. Insanity might have been the defence that she had used through the years to avoid the unpleasant consequences of her actions, and there truly was a degree of mental instability running through her as a result of her traumas and addictions, but none of it could sufficiently explain how she had come to that moment. Fingers steepled, smile on her face, watching the baby lying on the table spasmodically jerking as it desperately tried to draw air. Nothing could explain why she leaned in close to watch as the baby's face went pink, then red, and finally became purple and black as the blood being pumped to the brain found no path of escape because the veins had been closed by the pressure of the tape. Amelia Dyer had passed beyond the limits of our understanding as she sat there, watching and waiting for the eventual satisfaction of seeing the baby's frantic movements slow and then stop altogether. Waiting for the chest, at last, to cease its rise and fall. She held a finger in front of the baby's parted lips, just above where the swollen tongue now protruded and paused a moment to see if she could feel any hint of breath. She could not.

Finally, her daughter returned to the room and they bound both dead babies up, slipping them into the carpet bag, and Polly fetched in a couple of bricks that she had found in the alley out back so that the bag would sink when it hit the water.

In all her life, Polly had never seen her mother look happy or content. She had been born too late for that. By the time Amelia had moved on to husband number two, her whole face had contorted into a perpetual frown. But at that moment, looking on as her daughter prepared the babies' bodies for disposal, there was something akin to happiness in her mother's eyes. Some fierce and terrible joy in the horrific things that she had done.

That night, the 2nd of April, Amelia would depart once more from her daughter's home, taking first a bus, then a train back to Reading. All with her heavy carpet bag in tow.

Once she had arrived back at the town where she lived, she did not make a beeline for home as one might have expected. Instead, she cut across towards the river Thames, strolling along to the secluded area near to the Caversham Lock as the sun began to set late in the evening. Under cover of darkness, she approached the railings and began to shove the carpet bag through. It was too well stuffed with corpses and bricks to fit easily, and she spent several minutes wiggling it back and forth, becoming ever more distressed that someone might come along. Finally, the bag slipped between the iron railings and fell with a splash into the river. Amelia nodded to herself in satisfaction, knowing that the weighted bag would carry the bodies down into the depths and she would never have to think of them again. Turning, she was about to set off for home when she almost jumped out of her skin. There was a man there, out for an evening stroll, and he had seen her. How much he had seen, she could not say with certainty, but a dread was upon her now. So much so that she could not even give him an answer when he smiled and called out, 'Good Evening.'

She stormed off home in a fury, trying desperately to work out what could be done about this witness. How she could handle him, gain control over him, silence him before he could act against her. He was young enough that he wasn't liable to succumb to her wiles even if she threw herself at him. Polly was down in London and married off, so she couldn't have the girl flirt with him to turn his head. She didn't even know his name, though she knew his face. He was a resident in one of the other streets of Reading which made him a neighbour, technically. As she'd always been so intent on keeping to herself and avoiding attention, she wasn't sure which house, or even which street was his. She'd need to go out and find him the next day, she'd need to offer him something he couldn't refuse, money or... maybe he had some secret she could exploit to keep him quiet.

She was still stomping her way up the dirt path back to town when the fury and confusion began to leave her. The instability of her mind had become an ever-greater impediment to her as the years went by. The effects of her various traumas and addictions became cumulative, and she had long ago come to recognise that the snap decisions that she was making were not always the healthiest or the most helpful. She knew better, in her rational mind, than to act out of fear, so she made herself replay the scene she had just fled.

What could the man have really seen, even in the worst-case scenario? A woman pushing an old bag through a fence into the water. Was it a strange sight, worthy of comment? Yes, of course, but was it so strange that he'd be thinking twice about it in a week's time? No. If she went running up to him, offering him threats or money or anything else, then he'd have the memory burned into him, he'd know that something was truly wrong. But if she just let this pass unacknowledged, if she ignored the encounter, he'd likely forget all about it before too long. The bag was gone, sunken to the bottom of the river where it would never be seen again, and whatever was in that bag was gone, too. Even if the man had come to her with questions, she could just say it was an old, tattered bag she was throwing away. What was the worst trouble she could get in for disposing of some rubbish in the Thames? The river was practically an open sewer once you got downstream to London. She was hardly poisoning it by adding in one little bit of carpet scrap.

She had almost entirely calmed herself by the time she returned home to Granny Smith, who had been waiting for her with bated breath. There was no need to worry about what that man had seen at all.

The Prosecution

Doris Marmon and Harry Simmons were not the only babies that Amelia had disposed of in the Thames. Not by a long shot. But while she usually took all precautions with the disposal of bodies to avoid detection, there had been one situation in which she had been somewhat more hasty.

Helena Fry was fifteen months old by the time that she had come into Amelia's care at the Temple Meads Train Station on March 5th, but on the return back to her home in Reading, the baby was nowhere to be seen. All that Amelia had with her was a parcel wrapped in brown paper tucked under her arm.

She hid the parcel in one of the cupboards in her house, out of sight and out of mind. It didn't take long for a fetid aroma to be exuded. The pungent scent of decay. Amelia was nothing if not good at ignoring obvious problems, so she went on pretending that all was fine as the reek of death permeated every inch of her home, until finally, three weeks after she had first brought the corpse of Helena home with her, she decided it was time to be rid of it.

Typically, Amelia would have added weights to the package to ensure that it sank to the bottom of the river, but the smell was so powerful, even through the wrapping, that she couldn't convince herself to open it and add in some rocks. She reasoned that the body would be little but bones by now, and bones would sink, so there was no point in making matters even more disgusting if she could avoid it.

Carrying the body to her favourite disposal spot on the Thames, by the Caversham Lock, she did not need to take care, forcing it between the bars meant to keep pedestrians from slipping into the water by accident. Even at fifty-six, she still had strength enough in her arms to casually toss the corpse over the fence to splash down in the water while she vanished into the dark of the night. Returning home, she cracked open every window that she could to air the house out, and sat in the garden, hoping the stench might dissipate before she had to go to bed, but it seemed that the aroma would not depart so easily. Even days later, the place still reeked of death and decay.

Helena Fry did not sink. The brown paper parcel in which she was bound had contained the lighter-than-air gasses being released by decomposition so it immediately floated up to the surface of the Thames, bobbing its way slowly downriver. By dawn the next day, March 30th, it had scarcely made its way beyond the town proper when a bargeman travelling down towards London spotted it and retrieved it with a boat hook, thinking that it was something that had fallen overboard accidentally. It was only after getting the parcel on deck that he smelled the awful stench.

By all rights, he should have just tossed it back overboard, assuming it was some putrid rubbish that someone had tossed away, but something made him press on. Tying a handkerchief over his nose, he used a knife to cut the string holding the oddly shaped parcel shut and unravelled something that would haunt his nightmares every time he closed his eyes for the rest of his life.

The body was immediately turned over to the Reading Borough Police, and an enforced silence fell over the department. There were only three detectives on the force of Reading, none of whom were in any way equipped to deal with a sight as gruesome as the body of Helena Fry, so taken by decomposition by this point that it was barely recognisable as human. Despite feeling entirely out of their depth, Chief Constable Tewsley and Detective Constable Anderson went to work.

There was little in the way of identifiable marks on the body itself. A band of white tape tied tightly around the child's neck was easily recognisable as the cause of death, confirming that the baby had been murdered. Beyond that, there were none of the signs of abuse or neglect that would have been associated with the majority of child deaths. This was not the usual run-off from typical baby farmer operations. The baby had not become emaciated over a long period of time, it had been hale and healthy right up until the moment that it abruptly was not. Likewise, there were none of the indications of a shaken or beaten baby that would have suggested an abusive parent; the other primary suspects when it came to a baby's death in circumstances as grim as these.

Making matters even more complicated was the impossibility of identifying how long the baby had been in the water. Forensics was in its infancy, and making such a calculation was simply beyond the officers involved, they did not have the required knowledge base to make such a determination.

As such, anywhere upriver of Reading could easily have been the dump site. Swindon, Oxford, Dorchester, Wallingford and innumerable other villages, towns and cities were upriver. The baby might have been discarded like rubbish into the waters of the Thames, only to bob along the surface across the countryside, from any one of them Depending on where the baby had been dumped, they would have been looking at completely different dates on which it may have been dropped into the river, if a consistent speed of travel could even be calculated.

All of which is to say, despite the poor execution of her body disposal, Amelia had come upon a truly excellent forensic countermeasure all the same. One that could obscure not only her location but even the time of her murders.

In most cases, this would have been the end of the line for the investigation. No information was available that might progress matters, so it would have been abandoned after sending news of the discovery up to the other police forces along the length of the Thames. However, DC Anderson was not so willing to abandon little Helena Fry to an unmarked grave. Setting aside the body, he turned his attention instead to the sodden packaging that the baby had been wrapped in. Slowly drying it out over the course of the day, it eventually became firm enough to be handled. Then he began unfolding it. It was a plain sheet of brown paper, the kind found in businesses and homes across the country at the time. Nothing could have been less remarkable about it, and as a lead, it would lead nowhere. However, in amongst the folds of the paper, he did discover a label that had been attached to the parcel but had floated loose in the water, only brought up with the parcel by pure luck alone. A label from Temple Meads station in Bristol. This immediately provided them with a lead. Bristol was not upriver. It was many miles to the north, and while there would have been trains leading from there to the other towns upriver, the most direct route for this parcel to have gone into the river and been found in Reading was if it had been dumped in Reading after the train brought it there directly.

In itself, it wasn't enough to confirm anything at all, but it was progress, something that nobody had expected to make in this case. And it allowed them to begin piecing together a timeline, checking arrival times in Reading station coming from Bristol over the past week so that they might create windows of time in which the body may have been dumped after being brought to town.

The three weeks that Amelia had held onto the corpse blew a hole in that plan. Given that the baby's corpse was still more or less in one piece despite the state of decay, it was assumed that it had died shortly before being put into the water. The idea that someone might have sat with a dead body in their home for almost a month was so ridiculous that it didn't even occur to anyone involved in the investigation. As such, when they pulled the tickets from the train station to find out which locals arrived from Bristol, they completely failed to register Amelia at the beginning of the month.

Once more, the investigation should have ground to a complete halt were it not for the intervention of DC Anderson. While everyone else had gone tearing off to chase down any leads that the first piece of evidence had generated, he had remained on task with the brown paper that they'd recovered from the river, going over every inch of it, section by section, using a microscope.

It was only because of this obscene level of diligence that he was able to uncover the next piece of evidence that would ultimately result in the crime being solved. While the ink had washed away in the river, there was still an indentation in the paper where there had been writing on the brown paper's surface. Carefully tracing over this indentation, Anderson was able to copy what had originally been written on the package.

Mrs Thomas

26 Piggott's Road

Caversham

They had a name and an address tied to the murder now, and the next place that the investigating officers went flying off to as soon as they got word from DC Anderson was the village of Caversham, just a little to the north of Reading itself. There they found nobody by the name of Thomas at the address, with the prior tenant who had lived there never going by that name. At first, it seemed to be a dead end entirely, with whoever had been living here under a false name now having moved on, but then they got a chance to speak with some of the neighbours and another name for the mysterious Mrs Thomas did come up. Amelia Dyer.

It wasn't a name that meant anything to the local police. Amelia had entirely slipped under their radar when she moved into town, and all of the trouble that had followed her prior to her arrival in Reading had failed to catch up to her. Records were not shared across the various constabularies of the United Kingdom until almost a century later. What one town knew about a person would only come to another town's attention if those officers wrote to them requesting information and even then, it might take weeks before anyone found the time to do the requesting officers the courtesy of passing their files along. Many police departments were run like little fiefdoms by their Chief Constables, sharing nothing and treating other departments as competitors. Arguing about jurisdiction at every opportunity and caring more about inter-departmental politics than about actually solving crimes.

What luck that the mysterious figure of Amelia Dyer had not travelled so far as another jurisdiction then. A quick check of Reading town records uncovered her location at 45 Kensington Road, and plans were immediately set into motion to arrest her. Plans that were brought to an immediate halt by Chief Constable Tewsley.

While the young DC Anderson may have proven his expertise in detection and more than earned his paycheque for the month, he was still less experienced than Tewsley in terms of the actual psyche of the criminal. He had not pieced together nearly so swiftly the fact that all of the assumed identities and rapid address changes in Dyer's history indicated that she would be a serious flight risk if she caught wind of the police heading for her door. Reading was not so big a town that gossip wouldn't rapidly spread the moment that a warrant for Dyer's arrest was issued, and Tewsley knew without a doubt that rumours could run faster than his officers.

So instead, an alternate arrangement was made. A telegram was delivered to Amelia's house from a prospective client, a young woman who was unmarried had a newborn baby in need of care. She was in the local area and wanted to meet with Amelia to discuss the possibility of her 'fostering' the child. They intercepted the return telegram the same day, setting up a time for the meeting at Amelia's home on the morning of April 3rd.

This fake meeting served two purposes: firstly, proving beyond a shadow of a doubt that Amelia was involved in the practice of baby farming, and secondly, ensuring that Amelia's location was known.

When Amelia opened her door that morning to greet the young lady that the police had sent to serve as a decoy, she was immediately pounced upon by the officers hiding to either side of the door and placed immediately under arrest on suspicion of murder.

A search of the house turned up no infants, or even any remains of infants, but what the police uncovered did paint a horrifying picture of what had happened there all the same.

The stench of death still permeated every inch of the building. Rot, decay, and decomposition fouled the atmosphere of the entire house from top to bottom thanks to the little parcel that had been recovered from the Thames having been left in one of the cupboards for so long. What was missing in direct evidence tying her to the case was more than made up for in circumstantial evidence which painted a disturbingly graphic picture of the ghoulish deeds transpiring in the Dyer household.

White edging tape was found in abundance, though neither Amelia nor Granny Smith were in any way involved in the dressmaking trade. Laudanum and various other baby calming aids were around but given Amelia's long history of drug abuse that was hardly surprising. What they did not find was a single cot or baby. Nothing that you would expect to find at a baby farm because Amelia had graduated from running a farm long ago.

Now Amelia's time was spent operating nothing short of an abattoir.

There was ample supporting evidence of her grim trade. There were pawn tickets for a veritable hoard of children's clothing from shops all across the country. There were receipts for the advertisements that she had placed so many of the various local papers within her hunting grounds. There were letters from dozens of mothers requesting updates on the welfare of their children; all unanswered. Most damning of all were the telegrams. All of them clearly and openly referencing adoption arrangements, meeting places and times, and amounts to be paid for their baby to be taken away. There would have been ample enough evidence in the paper trail alone to convict Amelia of baby-farming if she was brought before the right kind of jury, but the absence of the babies that she was meant to be caring for rendered such charges moot, and opened up the possibility of the far worse crimes that she had been committing.

Judging by the paperwork alone, 'Mrs Thomas' had taken in over twenty babies from different people over the few months that she had been living in Reading. The same kind of mad frenzy of activity that had prompted her last move. Money was supposed to be her sole motivation for her actions, enough money to keep herself comfortable and out of the poor house permanently, but that motive gave way in the face of evidence of the volume of slaughter she was doling out. There was a small fortune in cash available to Amelia as a result of her many clients, but she had nothing that she wanted to spend it on. She was just hoarding it, doling it out sparingly to keep control of the people around her. If money had been her sole motivation, she could have retired on what she had. While this may make sense in retrospect, having seen the way that her murderous habit had developed into an addiction in itself, at the time the whole thing entirely baffled the police, who had never encountered this kind of murderer before.

Jack the Ripper was in operation in London at this time, slaughtering his way through the prostitutes of Whitechapel with abandon, and he would mark the first 'serial killer' as modern audiences would understand it. But the general population of the UK was not aware of enough details of that case to ascertain that his crimes were what was later known as 'passion killing,' driven not by some material gain, but by a carnal desire to do harm to others. The idea that there could be some psychological drive to murder was beyond the imaginings of most people of that period, and even those few who did entertain such thoughts were academics and philosophers rather than policemen. To them, all they could see was a series of irrational actions with no way of grasping what was happening in Amelia's mind to render such actions rational to her.

Twenty babies had been brought in, in quick succession, yet there was no trace of any one of them beyond the telegrams, letters and pawn tickets. No bodies, no babies, nothing.

At least Amelia seemed to have grasped that she was operating at far too fast a rate to avoid attention. The small part of her mind that remained rational and calculating had stepped in to protect her. Among the letters and telegrams were the inquiries that she had been making with landlords about an appropriately sized house in Somerset, where she had been planning to move next. If the police had not leapt into action immediately upon the discovery of Helena Fry rather than conducting the usual plodding investigation of a dead body, in all likelihood Amelia would have slipped through their fingers and continued on to kill and kill again.

The remainder of April 3rd proved to be an unpleasant experience for everyone involved. They could not draw a confession out of Amelia regarding the baby's body that they had found, nor could she simply stonewall her way out of this situation. But without a confession, all that the police had to convict her with was circumstantial evidence. No witness had yet come forward, and they didn't even know which of the various babies that Amelia had taken into her 'care' had been the one discovered bobbing along the Thames. The detectives working the case were drowned in all the paperwork from her home. There were so many individual pieces of evidence that it was overwhelming to carefully search through everything. Despite her chaotic behaviour in other regards, she had been meticulous in keeping all her correspondence. Perhaps it represented some sort of trophy to remind herself of the murders that she had committed, or possibly it was simply a holdover from when her lifestyle was a little more legal.

Amelia was officially remanded into custody on the murder charges on April 4th and would never see the light of day again.

In the days that followed her arrest, the local police were sanctioned to dredge the river to look for any other evidence. Over the course of the month, the entire riverbed was scraped for evidence and a further six dead bodies were discovered in and around Amelia's favourite dumping site. Judging by the state of decay, they were all recent. Of course, there was always the possibility that any less recent bodies she may have dumped in the river had degraded beyond the point of recovery. That said, Amelia had not lived in Reading for all that long by this point in time, so it is quite possible that the six corpses of infants recovered from the riverbed represented every single one of the babies that she'd taken in since moving into the area, and all her prior victims had found their way to other dump sites elsewhere around the country.

Around the throats of every one of those babies, bar one, was a tight knot of white edging tape. A cohesive thread connecting all the murders to a single perpetrator. Another damning piece of circumstantial evidence given the discovery of so much edging tape in Amelia's home during the search.

Still, no confession was forthcoming from Amelia, although she had now realised that this was not a situation she was going to be able to talk herself out of after a few days of repeated questioning. She began to present herself in interviews as though she were mentally unstable – something that did not require much in the way of acting chops – and began laying the foundation for some sort of insanity defence for her actions. Inspired by and emulating her own mother's mental deterioration that Amelia had witnessed in her childhood, one of the aspects that Amelia latched onto was religious mania. She began praying at every opportunity, calling out to God as though he were in the room with her and was going to save her. Claiming that everything she did was in accordance with his plan. At no point throughout her life had Amelia ever been known to attend church of her own accord. During those periods when she was in the poorhouse, she was forced to go to church and her true feelings about that had been clearly expressed with much eye-rolling and a general attitude of contempt for the whole subject of religion. It is likely that her aversion stemmed from her earliest childhood exposure to religion in the form of her mother's deranged prayers being shouted through the house in the middle of the night.

Yet even this didn't seem to convince the police that she was not responsible for her actions or that, should she offer up a confession, it could not be taken as credible. Too much of her behaviour over the years had been quite obviously calculating and coldly deliberate. As they began to build a file on her history across the country through ongoing contact with other constabularies, they realised that this 'insanity' was actually a recurring pattern of behaviour that surfaced each time she was confronted with scrutiny by the authorities. They read about her numerous stays in bedlam houses, always coinciding with the police closing in on her previous criminal enterprises, and finally came upon the details of her laudanum-drinking escape from justice.

Immediately, a constable rose from the offices and ran to the jail in Reading where she was being held pending transfer to a more permanent home in a larger prison. Bursting into her cell with the warden in tow, the men arrived just in time to catch her as she swung from a noose made of bedsheets, hanging herself from the end of her upturned bed frame.

If forensics had been more advanced at the time, the doctor's examination of her injuries might have revealed that she had only been hanging there for a fraction of a second, having jumped from the bucket used as her toilet only when she heard someone about to open the door. But regardless of whether this was just another ploy to make herself look insane, or a genuine suicide attempt, she was treated as a suicide risk all the same and kept under near-constant surveillance for so long as she was in Reading Gaol.

There would be one more suicide attempt later, once again foiled by swift action from the guards, but there was no doubt in anyone's mind that the second was even more bogus than the first. Amelia had known her guard's schedule and when she would be checked on, scheduling her attempted strangulation to precisely coincide with the guard looking in on her and thereby guaranteeing her safety. Now that the pattern of behaviour had been recognised, the shock value of a woman attempting to take her own life had been lost.

It probably also helped that everyone was considerably more shocked by her crimes than by her later actions.

During her stay in jail pending the prosecution moving forward, the police had worked their way through the multitudes of single mothers who had been in correspondence with Amelia. They repeatedly assured the women that they were not in any trouble for what they had done, and promised not to speak openly of what had transpired so that they could be assured of full witness cooperation. From there it was simply a matter of matching dead bodies to parents.

Evelina Marmon was able to identify her daughter Doris. The only child without the strip of white tape around its neck. Harry Simmons was similarly identified by his mother despite the deformity that death had inflicted upon his once peaceful little face. Rounding out the group was the mother of Helena Fry, who was able to identify the first body that had been recovered as that of her daughter, though she chose to remain anonymous after making that identification and would not speak at trial.

Both of those mothers would be brought to Reading Gaol to look through the bars at Amelia Dyer and answer the deciding question of the matter. Was this the woman that they had turned their baby over to, with the promise that it would be taken care of and raised?

Both women gave a different name for the woman behind bars; Ms Marmon called her Mrs Harding, and Ms Simmons called her Mrs Thomas. But more importantly, both of them positively identified Amelia as the one who had taken their children.

For Evelina Marmon, it had been eleven days since she last saw her daughter alive and well. Eleven days, in which she had reached out twice to Amelia Dyer for assurances that everything was well, with one of her attempts entirely ignored and the other promptly replied to by telegram, informing her that little Doris was settling in well and enjoying the country air that she had never had the opportunity to breathe.

At about this time, Amelia's neighbour from Reading came forward to tell his odd tale of a carpet bag being pushed through the bars and into the river in the dead of night, having finally made the connection between what he had seen and the stories that were now circulating about bodies in the water. It was exactly this eye-witness testimony that the courts would rely on to take things forward. All the circumstantial evidence in the world meant nothing without a means to directly tie Amelia Dyer to the bodies, and now they had that link.

Still, a confession from Amelia would seal the deal, and the fact that she was now coming to realise that there would be no getting out of this one with feigned nervous breakdowns or invented crises, brought them that little bit closer to success in extracting one from her. All that they needed now was one last push to get her across the finish line.

They had tracked her white tape back to her daughter and made the obvious connection. If the use of the tape as a murder weapon had originated in her daughter's company, that meant that more than likely, murders had occurred under her daughter's roof. With her knowledge.

Both Polly and her husband Arthur were arrested on suspicion of acting as accomplices in Amelia's murder and disposal of the babies. Their home was searched for evidence and their lives were irrevocably upended. Both immediately lost their jobs as a result of their arrest and any standing that they had managed to build up among society and their peers was wiped away in an instant.

The trouble with putting pressure on Amelia Dyer was that she had nothing to lose. She had spent her whole life on the precipice of despair and death, so there was nothing that she could be threatened with that would actually scare her into action. But her daughter Polly, her beloved daughter and the only family that she remained in contact with had everything to lose. She had made a life for herself after crawling free of her mother's immensely dark shadow. She had built that life predicated on the assumption of other people that she was as normal and upstanding as any of the rest of them. To Polly, the destruction of her reputation would be as devastating as any hangman's noose.

They couldn't hurt Amelia, but Polly was not nearly so hardened to suffering. Even the threat of her husband's death was enough to break her. And from there it was just a matter of letting her meet with her mother and sob her eyes out.

Amelia did not care about anyone, except for herself and Polly, so the police went after that point of weakness and got everything that they wanted. Amelia made a full confession, offering to accept full responsibility for the fate of any of the bodies found in the water that had the white tape tied around their necks. That was her signature. Her daughter had provided her with the tape entirely unwittingly, with no idea what she intended to do with it. Amelia went on to assert that Polly's husband Arthur was as ignorant a man as any she had ever met and was none the wiser about any of it, so hanging him would do as much to improve society as hanging a random donkey in the street.

On April 16th of 1896, Amelia penned a confession to be sent to the inquest that had been raised to answer for the dead babies that had been discovered. It read:

'Sir will you kindly grant me the favour of presenting this to the magistrates on Saturday the 18th instant I have made this statement out, for I may not have the opportunity then I must relieve my mind I do know and I feel my days are numbered on this earth but I do feel it is an awful thing drawing innocent people into trouble I do know I shal have to answer before my Maker in Heaven for the awful crimes I have committed but as God Almighty is my judge in Heaven a on Hearth neither my daughter Mary Ann Palmer nor her husband Alfred Ernest Palmer I do most solemnly declare neither of them had any thing at all to do with it, they never knew I contemplated doing such a wicked thing until it was to late I am speaking the truth and nothing but the truth as I hope to be forgiven, I myself and I alone must stand before my Maker in Heaven to give an answer for it all.

Witnes my hand,
Amelia Dyer.'

Whether it was haste, the decline of her mental faculties, or some attempt at playing dumb that led Amelia to write with so many errors is unclear. What does appear obvious, though, is that the liberal use of religious references was likely a calculated attempt to influence the opinion of the presiding judge. It was probably meant to encourage him to view her with some degree of empathy and kindness. Perhaps it was also a ploy designed to convince him that, however, damaged or corrupted she had become, her core belief system was once moral and based on Christian values, despite all the evidence to the contrary suggesting she had never had a single moral in her entire life.

Arthur Palmer was discharged as a result of this letter, but Polly remained in custody. While it was possible that neither of the Palmers were aware of Amelia's activities, it was considered extremely unlikely that she could have committed all her crimes alone, given the sheer scale of activity. Granny Smith was still being charged as an accessory but clearly lacked the mental capacity to have been much more than a dogsbody. The fact that they were in serious trouble yet Amelia had shown no care whatsoever for the poor woman that she'd supposedly taken off the streets out of pure kindness, was a testament to how unimportant she was in the scheme of things. Smith was, at best, a mere afterthought to Amelia.

This lack of care proved very helpful to the prosecution's case. The scorned woman provided testimony that would damn herself as well as Amelia in exchange for a promise of a lighter sentence for her complicity, and to spite Amelia who, throughout all their time together, had never treated her with the slightest bit of kindness unless she wanted something.

With everything that was required for an open and shut case against Amelia, the police transferred her to a holding cell in London to await her trial, but given how sensational the case was, it did not take long before it was on the docket.

On May 22nd Amelia made her first appearance at the Old Bailey Courthouse in London, to enter her plea. In the case of Doris Marmon, the only one of the murders that she was currently being charged with thanks to the continuation of evidence from start to finish making it the easiest to prosecute, she pleaded guilty to the premeditated murder of the baby.

Over the following days, her family and associates all came out to testify against her, talking about their mounting suspicions of where all her money came from and about some of the sinister behaviour that they had witnessed her engaging in.

Not one person spoke out in her defence because there was no sort of defence that could be made for her actions.

Evelina Marmon came forward and entered her sorry tale into the record, speaking of how she had so desperately loved and wanted the daughter that Amelia had stolen from her, and how she had only ever wanted someone to care for the baby in the short term until she had saved enough to provide for the two of them.

Afterwards came the testimony of the man who had seen her dropping the bodies into Caversham Lock, presented as a means to tie her to the disposal of Doris' body. This was followed by testimony from the officers who had discovered the weighted carpetbag and its grisly contents.

Both the start and end of the story of Doris Marmon's murder had been told to the court, and many felt that, in itself, would have been enough. But then Polly took the stand, looking down into her mother's eyes, she filled in the middle section. Describing how her mother had come to her house in London, sought out the white edging tape that Polly used in her dressmaking, and then was left alone with the baby who stopped crying soon after, never to be heard again.

The fact that her own daughter was willing to testify against her was utterly damning to the minds of the jury. Even if they hadn't already been entirely convinced by the various character witnesses establishing that Amelia had been involved in the criminal enterprise of baby farming for a long time, the fact that her own flesh and blood was ready to come out and provide evidence that proved in everyone's minds that her mother was guilty was a testament to her evil.

What may have escaped the jury's attention at this time, due to the heightened emotions surrounding this case, was that every family member and close acquaintance who testified against Amelia stood to benefit from her conviction substantially. Every single one of them was under suspicion of involvement in her crimes, and it was vital to them that she shouldered the full blame for everything that she had done so that they might avoid any culpability. Amelia Dyer was going to hang, one way or another. They just wanted to make sure that they didn't end up swinging in the breeze beside her.

Polly, in particular, probably wouldn't have been so vocal and direct about everything if her mother hadn't specifically instructed her to be so. She was still on the hook for involvement in the many various murders that had occurred in her home, and unless the full blame could be transferred over to Amelia, then it was entirely possible that she'd share her mother's fate and infamy.

Although Amelia's confession had exonerated him, it was still in Arthur's interest to make sure that she received the full burden of guilt. Otherwise, the wife that he loved was liable to be snatched away from him. As for Granny Smith, in the back of her somewhat addled mind was the idea that if Amelia was out of the picture, she'd be set to inherit everything from her. She could take over Amelia's criminal empire and enjoy the fruits of her labour for the first time. This was not to be the case, but this along with other delusions, such as the possibility of walking away scot-free after her ongoing involvement in the day-to-day operations of the baby farm-turned-slaughterhouse, was more than enough motive for her to do everything in her power to convince the jury of Amelia's guilt as well as her full control over the whole situation.

One might have expected Amelia to fight all of this. To rail against the relentless tide of very real betrayals that she now faced with the same vitriol as she had railed against all the imagined betrayals throughout the years. But nothing could be further from the truth. She nodded approvingly to her friends and family as they took the stand and described her evil. She wanted this. She wanted all of the blame to be pinned on her because she believed that despite everything, there was still a way out, and if she was going to be successfully dodging bullets today, she wanted every single gun pointed her way.

She had pled guilty to the murder, conceded that everything had gone exactly as the prosecution described it and sat calmly throughout the whole thing, fully expecting to escape the consequences with one simple trick. Precisely the same trick that she had been pulling since the very beginning of her criminal career. She meant to be found not guilty by reason of insanity.

The prosecutors had been prepared for this eventuality by the police. They had been thoroughly briefed on the way that Amelia had suddenly switched tactics during her interrogations, and on the manner in which she had used 'nervous breakdowns' and suicide attempts in the past to avoid facing the consequences for her actions and to sidestep investigation. The prosecutors had come prepared with doctors who had assessed Amelia's condition, doctors who were prepared to stake their professional credibility on the line and say without a shadow of a doubt that she was sane enough to know the difference between right and wrong. Sane enough to premeditate every one of her crimes, to operate a complex conspiracy involving dozens of moving parts, utilize multiple false identities and organize multiple points of contact with her victims. There was nothing to suggest a disorganised mind as one might find in the insane – at least to the standards of the time. So it was that her attempts to argue that she was insane, and to prove it in court with her overblown and exaggerated actions all came to nothing. Worse still, in her attempts to paint herself as cartoonishly deranged, she revealed terrible facts about how she had conducted the wholesale slaughter of her young victims. About the way that she had killed them slowly and savoured every moment. About the ways that she had disposed of the bodies like they were nothing. Nobody did more harm to Amelia Dyer's case than Amelia Dyer. All attempts at discounting herself due to alleged insanity were thrown out, and instead of being tarred with the brush of the mad, she was instead marked by every member of the jury as the most heinous personification of evil.

It took the jury exactly four and a half minutes to decide Amelia's fate. To decide that she had to die for what she had done. Less time than it took the babies that she strangled to finally pass out. At least she was not kept in suspense. With the verdict handed down, there was no question that the judge would sentence her to death by hanging. The harshest punishment available to him, but still somehow nowhere near sufficient given the crimes that she had committed.

As to the question of why she had not been tried for all of the other murders, they were considered by the state to be a moot point once the conviction and subsequent death sentence had taken place. There was no point in wasting more of the court's time. Everyone involved, from investigators to family of the victims now knew the truth of the matter, and that justice was being served, so there would have been no point in dragging it all through court. Also, by holding back all of the other crimes to try later, the crown would have been able to take multiple shots at gaining a conviction against Amelia if the first had somehow failed.

It had not. As a result, she was going to die within a month.

After the court was adjourned, Amelia was taken directly to Newgate Prison, where she was kept isolated from the general population, many of whom had something of a bone to pick with a woman who may have killed upwards of four hundred babies if the more lavish accounts in the newspapers were correct. There was a specific wing of the prison set aside for those awaiting execution, a quiet wing with regular visits from the prison chaplain being about the only thing breaking up the monotony of the long hours of waiting.

At her request, Amelia was furnished with some blank journals which she slowly but steadily filled with a full account of her life and her crimes. An extended confession of sorts that could be read after she was gone in case there had been any detail that she had missed when testifying.

Through the three weeks between her conviction and execution, Amelia had absolutely no concern for her well-being. Instead, she remained entirely fixated on what would happen to her daughter Polly, who still had to stand trial.

Amelia was subpoenaed to appear as a witness in Polly's trial by her daughter's defence attorney but given that the trial was not set to occur until after Amelia's execution, the state was placed in something of an awkward position. They could delay Amelia's execution so that she could attend to other legal matters, but this would set a dangerous precedent that would allow criminals to deliberately embroil themselves in other cases as a way to avoid their just punishment. The matter ended up in the High Courts of the land, with the decision finally being reached that, legally, Amelia could not be called as a witness because she was already dead. Legally she became dead the moment that the judge sentenced her to death, and the fact that her body was still pumping blood and wandering around was a mere technicality that was to be overlooked until the mistake was corrected.

Amelia's appearance at her daughter's trial could have gone either way, in terms of helping the defence. She certainly hadn't done anything to ingratiate herself to the jury in her case, and her bizarre and outlandish behaviour might very well have soured whatever goodwill Polly had managed to scrape together. However, she remained the only witness who could speak to the actual perpetrator of all her crimes, given that there had been no survivors of them.

So even now, her lengthy confession written across the pages of no less than five journals was not being written out of altruism so that the victims' families might find peace, but so that they could be used as evidence in her daughter's defence. Amelia had sacrificed her own life to ensure that all the crimes were pinned to her and her alone, and she certainly wasn't going to let a little thing like death interfere with her plans.

With her full confessions completed, there was nothing left for Amelia to do except wait for her fate to finally arrive. The days ticked by like minutes, with nothing for Amelia to do but stare at her cell walls and read her confessions. Like she was deliberately trying to make her life flash before her eyes one last time before she died.

Up until the final moments of her life, she was still consumed by the anxiety that had plagued her since her early childhood of servitude. She could find no rest, even knowing that on the dawn of the next day, she would be going to eternal peace with no more concern for worldly affairs at all.

It was the night of Tuesday, the 9th of June 1896, when the Newgate chaplain approached her one final time to ask if she wished to be absolved of her sins. Of course she did, she told him. She wouldn't have been here otherwise, she would have pled not guilty and gotten off scot-free if she hadn't wanted this awful burden lifted. With that in mind, he asked if she wished to make a confession so that she might receive his absolution. She handed him the journals and asked, "Isn't this enough?"

Amelia received her last rites, in as much as they could be performed on someone who was showing no interest in them, but despite this, no weight was lifted from her shoulders and she paced on and on into the depths of the night. Absolution of her immortal soul had done nothing to abate her fears, because despite all of the noises she may have been making, she had no faith in anything or anyone but herself. There was only one thing left in the world that she cared about at all.

The warden came to visit her just before midnight, and she assumed that it was to gloat, or some part of the usual proceedings. It was not. He had received word from court that the charges against Polly had been dropped, and she had been released back out into the world.

Amelia collapsed onto her cot, all the strength and tension leaving her body in one great rush. Finally, it was over. Finally, throwing herself on her sword had proven to be worth it. Polly would go free, she would live on, and some part of Amelia would continue on after she had died. Not in the spiritual sense, but in the physical. Her daughter was not going to pay for her crimes, and so with that burden finally removed and that good news nestled in her heart, she curled up on her cot and fell into a deep and dreamless sleep for perhaps the first time in her adult life.

She was roused in the morning at eight o'clock and marched out into the yard a half hour later once her morning ablutions were completed. She was accompanied by the attendant chaplain, though the two seemed to have nothing to say to one another, and a guard to ensure that no attempt at escape was made. James Billington, the patriarch of a famous family of executioners was in attendance as her hangman, carefully preparing the gallows to the precise specifications that he had decided were the best to ensure a clean execution, and then finally, just before the allotted time of nine a.m, Amelia was brought up onto the gallows and asked if she had any last words that she wished to share.

She shrugged her shoulders and said, "I have nothing to say." Something of an anticlimax, given how fond of her own voice she seemed to have grown during the court proceedings.

A black burlap bag was placed over her head, followed by the noose, which was then tightened into place around her neck. She was positioned on the trap door of the gallows, which would give away with the pull of a lever, and all fell silent until the allotted moment arrived on Billington's watch, at which point he pulled the lever and watched her fall with the very same obsessive intensity that she had watched all of the babies that she strangled to death. Billington was a perfectionist, obsessed with his work beyond the point of all reason. He had practised and experimented with mocked-up gallows before he had ever found employment as a hangman, trying out different lengths of rope, weights and dummies so that he could always ensure that he got the best, cleanest kills. As such, Amelia's death was the absolute antithesis of the awful murders that she had committed, while still being technically carried out by similar means. When the lever was pulled and the weight of her body carried her down, it was not to dangle and spin for minutes at a time waiting for all the air to be drawn from her lungs and her brain to die in a haze of agony and darkness. When she fell, there was a sudden drop, and then a sudden sharp jerk as the noose took hold, snapping her neck in an instant and killing her immediately.

The prison bell had been tolling throughout the whole procedure and would go on to toll another fifteen minutes, as was customary. The crowds that were gathered outside of the prison yard were unable to see inside and did not know the exact moment of Amelia's death, nor could they come and gawk at the notorious murderer finally being murdered herself. But they did receive some satisfaction. A cheer went up when a black flag was run up the flagpole atop the prison walls to inform the world that an execution had taken place. Her death certificate was read to the gathered masses outside the gates of the prison and then pinned to the board there so that anyone who wished to observe it could come and check the details, assuring themselves that the monster was dead, and the evil of Amelia Dyer was finally over.

Finally, the campaign of horror that she had conducted all her life had come to an end with her death. No more babies would be taken away and murdered for profit. Except, it wasn't over. Not even close.

The Ogress

Amelia Dyer's demise was only the beginning of sweeping reforms to adoption laws in Victorian Britain. Restrictions were greatly tightened to prevent anything like this from happening again, with every change in 'ownership' of a child would now be required by law to be registered with the local authorities. All of the existing organisations that helped to operate adoptions were placed under scrutiny, with the Salvation Army, in particular, suffering a heavy blow to their reputation when it was discovered that they may have inadvertently endorsed Amelia Dyer.

Newspaper personal advertisements were scoured daily by the police, searching for anything that might resemble a baby farmer and jumping on every opportunity to make arrests, sometimes even catching those who were legitimately just attempting to make real adoptions.

The scandal of Amelia Dyer's very existence was enough to shame the whole of society; but instead of blame laying where it belonged, on those demanding an unreasonable standard of 'purity,' there was instead a massive puritanical drive in response to news of her crimes. These babies would not have existed and been put into vulnerable positions were it not for the sinful behaviour of the lower classes, bringing children into the world that they couldn't afford to raise, or worse yet, bringing them into the world outside of wedlock. All of the conditions that had made the world ripe for someone like Amelia Dyer to come along were exacerbated rather than addressed, with the ones receiving the harshest punishments not being the baby farmers who were exploiting the very real and desperate need for adoption services, but the people who were trying to rehome a child. The sentences handed down to baby farmers may have been tremendous even by the standards of the time, but they were, as a rule, professional criminals who knew how to avoid police detection. The individuals who needed their services were not nearly so competent, so typically they were the ones to suffer the consequences of the more draconian laws.

A fledgling organisation, The National Society for the Prevention of Cruelty to Children, was still in its infancy when the Dyer case went to trial, little more than a tiny consortium of concerned citizens who were doing their best to stem the tide of depravity and horror being inflicted upon the innocent. With Amelia's conviction, they saw a sudden rise to prominence and power. They had been founded in 1884, but their profile suddenly leapt as a result of the Dyer case, and they soon had so much funding that they were able to employ inspectors to work alongside the police and existing social services – such as they were – to ensure that children were not being sold and traded like cattle. Their campaigns and lobbying would do a great deal to improve matters for the youth of Victorian Britain, leading to a gradual improvement in their living conditions as well as their working conditions. Eventually, their efforts coupled with those of fledgling trade unions resulted in the formation of laws preventing children from being forced into the workforce by poverty at all. Ironically, some good came out of what Amelia had done in that the abject horror of realising what had been happening right under the noses of society drove it to improve, to prevent the exact same tragedy from repeating all over again, and to fight back against any of the myriad other potential tragedies that plagued the life of impoverished youths.

Yet despite all the good work and goodwill that these campaigns generated, two years after Amelia's execution the baby farming trade was still alive and well. So much so that railway workers had now been instructed to examine any packages being transported on their trains that were of approximately the same size as a human baby. Which, in the grand scheme of things turned out to be a frankly ridiculous percentage of them. During one of these now routine inspections at Newton Abbot Station in Devon, one of the workers was horrified to discover that the soft paper-wrapped package in his hands was, in fact, a baby. A three-week-old baby, soaking wet and so cold to the touch that before ripping the parcel open, the worker assumed she was dead. But despite all that she'd suffered through, the baby in the parcel was still breathing. She was rushed to the nearest hospital where she received proper treatment and fully recovered. Only then did the true grimness of the railway worker's discovery begin to be realised by everyone in town. The baby's mother, as it turned out, was a widow by the name of Jane Hill who lived in Plymouth. She had, only the morning before the baby's discovery on the train, handed the child over with all the official paperwork correctly filled out, to a woman by the name of Mrs Stewart. A younger woman who had agreed to foster the child for the very reasonable one-off fee of twelve pounds.

This Mrs Stewart was never tracked down due to it being a false name that seemed to lead nowhere, but everything about the physical description of the baby farmer led the authorities to an inescapable conclusion. The woman who had passed herself off as an adoptive mother was, in fact, Polly Dyer.

There was not enough evidence to convict her, and it literally took months before authorities could track her down anyway, by which point any solid evidence that she actually had been running a baby farm had long since vanished. But all the same, the fact remained that she had been cleared of all wrongdoing in her mother's crimes yet now appeared to be carrying them on for her. Albeit with less brutality and competence.

Because of how sensational the case was in the press, Polly had legally changed her name as well as her residence repeatedly, but it seemed that the spectre of her mother would never fully leave her. Even if she had not been described so accurately by Jane Hill, the assumption that she was a baby killer would have followed her to the ends of the earth all the same.

The sensation created by the discovery of Amelia's crimes had led to many different names being given to her in the papers, and even more, were concocted by the common people of Britain. Calling her the Reading Baby Farmer, The Angel Maker, and most commonly, the Ogress of Reading.

The latter name was immortalised in a popular ballad at the time. It is a song that circulated so popularly in taverns that we still have accounts of it to this day:

'The old baby farmer, the wretched Miss Dyer.

At Old Bailey her wages is paid.

In times long ago, we'd 'a' made a big fire.

And roasted so nicely that wicked old jade.'

Speculation abounded about just how many innocent children had lost their lives to Amelia's cruelty. Taking into account the length of time that she was operating her various baby farms and using the number of children that she had killed in the time surrounding the discovery of Helen Fry, papers had estimated she had a body count of around four hundred. It is likely that this number is grossly exaggerated considering the fact that she did not consistently kill at the same rate throughout the entirety of her criminal career. Whenever she felt the weight of suspicion was on her, she would halt her operations entirely for weeks or sometimes months at a time, even going into a Bedlam House when she felt the heat was especially high. This resulted in vast periods of time when she would not have been able to commit any crimes at all. Additionally, her stints in the poorhouse and in prison would have contributed to significant periods of time when she would have been under intense observation and scrutiny.

If she had committed all four hundred of the murders that she was accused of at the time, then she would be one of the most prolific serial killers in human history. That being said, in all likelihood, she probably only dispatched half that many at the most generous of estimates. The actual number of her victims is impossible to irrefutably verify but is unlikely to have broken into three figures.

The fundamental problem was not that Amelia Dyer was capable of killing all of those children. The problem was that she lived in a society where between one and four hundred babies could entirely disappear from existence without society as a whole being in any way aware of it. There were no safeguards in place for Victorian England's most vulnerable. The only assistance that those in poverty or bad situations could hope for amounted to little more than thinly disguised punishments or outright enslavement in the poorhouses. As a society, the Victorians had decided that they were too moral to tolerate children born out of wedlock. They intended to punish both the mothers and their children out of existence to prove a point. Amelia was simply the mechanism by which that punishment was meted out.

Among those extremists of social sciences, there are the social Darwinists, who believe that society is improved by the removal of 'weak' or 'inferior' people. For many such people, the modern criminal known as a serial killer represents a kind of societal immune system. Picking off those victims that society as a whole does not care about, the poor and the homeless, those who operate outside of the boundaries of what 'polite society' allows. In a way, Amelia Dyer is perfectly representative of their viewpoint on serial killers. She served exactly the function described; killing those that society wanted gone, without any sort of draconian laws having to be passed that enforced their extermination.

In the cases of many, if not most serial killers, the fact that the killer is preying upon those that society cares about the least leads to their crimes being investigated with considerably less diligence or fervour than they deserve, and in Amelia Dyer's case that was likely the truth. As much as there was a great deal of upset and handwringing over the deaths of the many children in her care, there was no small portion of Victorian society that felt that her actions were – if not justified – then at least acceptable, as they addressed the fundamental problem of the immorality of the lower classes. There were plenty of wealthy, well-connected aristocrats who wished that they could do much the same as Amelia Dyer, but on a grander scale, to effectively wipe away the poor and destitute instead of having to foot the tawdry bill to ensure their ongoing survival by way of taxes and charity.

When society at large decides that an entire subsection of the population is subhuman, it is only a matter of time until the consequence is extermination. We have seen this time and time again throughout history, and the fact that the governing powers of Victorian England were not directly responsible for the execution of the babies does nothing to remove guilt from them. The world is always going to have bad people in it, regardless of how perfect a society they live in, but in a well-constructed society, the individual's ability to do catastrophic damage is limited. Mitigation of damage is the reason that many countries have gun control and that even in countries where it is perfectly legal to own a firearm, it is not legal to own a thermonuclear bomb. At some point, one person will break down and do something unconscionable, but if society is built correctly, the amount of damage that they can inflict before they are caught is minimized.

In Amelia's case, there was no limit to the harm that she could do. The systems that were in place in her time actively encouraged her behaviour instead of preventing it. She was financially rewarded for the massacre of innocent babies whose only crimes were being born outside of conventional marriages.

The mothers were the ones who were meant to be punished for their immorality, and the fact that it was the babies who suffered was typically considered an unfortunate side effect. Through the use of baby farms, it was felt that the mothers were passing on the burden of their sins to the children, abandoning the unfortunate children to suffer in the mother's place as she should have suffered, while unfairly allowing her to carry on with her life. After considerable reflection and debate, two 'moral' factions sprang up with somewhat different viewpoints. One side felt that the death of infants constituted an unconscionable and intolerable evil, and the other side felt that the deaths were an acceptable loss serving to punish the immoral lower classes and that allowing the mothers of said babies to avoid having their offspring attached to them like millstones for the rest of their life would do nothing but encourage more immoral behaviour in the future. Of course, such a clear-cut dichotomy of opinions rarely reflects the true feelings of any society. In reality, there was a blending of both sets of beliefs culminating in a wide variety of responses to Amelia Dyer's crimes. Regardless, one point could be agreed upon. The baby farming had to be stopped. Accordingly, massive clampdowns on easy adoptions and intense scrutiny of all parties involved in adoptions became foundational in the development of social care for children in the UK. There was considerable public outcry expressing widespread disgust and dismay that such atrocities could have been happening right under the noses of the police for over a decade without anyone intervening. Never mind that there had been countless inquests into baby farming. Never mind that the royal family had commissioned their own doctor to investigate the deaths caused by laudanum and opiate baby-soothers, and into how they were routinely abused by baby farmers. When all these things were at a low boil in the background of society, they were ignored. It was only when someone like Amelia Dyer came along and was blatant in her slaughter that the problem could no longer be swept under the rug. In a way, this was a positive outcome to her awful crimes, as the practice of baby farming did go into decline following her execution and the example that had been made of her. But an industry going into decline is not the same as it disappearing entirely, and despite all the changes that were made in Dyer's wake, elements of the same practices that she and others indulged in would be seen time and time again throughout history, even into the modern era.

So, the question remains; what was wrong with Amelia Dyer? The doctors of her time judged her to be sane and competent enough to stand trial for her actions. She was deemed rational in spite of the fundamentally irrational things that she did out of a fear of poverty, and out of her bizarre lust for slaughter. There were fundamental currents of irrational behaviour expressed throughout her life spawning the belief by some that she had inherited some degree of madness from her mother, despite the fact that her mother's condition was the result of brain damage rather than genetic factors. The question of nature vs. nurture has sometimes been brought into the debate. The idea has been considered that simply spending time with someone who was insane at an impressionable age was enough to do permanent damage to Amelia's psyche.

There can be no question that her psychological problems were rooted in the trauma of her early life, but the world is full of people who have had traumatic incidents in their past without turning into mass murderers. All her siblings grew up to be normal, outstanding citizens despite having been raised in the same situation, albeit none of them being consigned to the full-time role of housekeeper and caretaker as Amelia had been. So, perhaps there was something fundamentally different in Amelia's makeup that meant that where the others had merely bent under the weight of what they had witnessed, she snapped. We will never know precisely what was going on inside her head, even with careful examination of the journals she left behind, because everything that she wrote or said about her crimes was deliberately constructed to present a specific persona; a carefully cultivated image that might have led to her being found innocent of the awful things that she'd done. But such behaviour is, in itself, quite telling. Even the most hardened of psychopaths will usually abandon their fiction and fabrication in the end and allow themselves to be seen, but for Amelia, such a thing was impossible. As though her behaviour was not simply constructed for the purposes of manipulation but was pathological. If true, that begs the next question: If she were to be tried in a modern court, would she still have been considered sane?

It is not possible to diagnose a dead woman with a mental illness. No doctor would do so. But for the purposes of speculation, we can discuss one particular disorder which could blend with Amelia Dyer's circumstances and create a perfect storm.

Borderline personality disorder has historically been underdiagnosed and poorly understood, even by medical professionals. When that diagnosis was given, it would frequently be accompanied with the sense that it was a social 'death sentence' because there was no known treatment or cure. Among the many thousands of women treated for 'hysteria' over the centuries, no small number would have been suffering from BPD, and as we now know, the 'treatments' for hysteria ranged from the torturous to the nonsensical.

The key factor in borderline personality disorder is emotional instability. An inability to properly regulate one's own emotional state. There are various other factors, but the core experience of someone suffering from BPD is that life is like a roller coaster full of constant and drastic ups and downs. Everything is the greatest that it has ever been, or everything is the worst it has ever been. They feel like they could take on the world or they feel like they should just die.

BPD can first be diagnosed in adolescence but is typically only addressed later because many of the traits that make up the condition are far easier to recognise in an adult person, rather than a child. Typically there is a consistency in the sufferer's experiences throughout their lives, from that first manifestation of their symptoms all the way through diagnosis and beyond. In modern psychiatry, cognitive behavioural therapy has shown some great success in treating BPD, breaking the patterns of thought and behaviour that characterise the condition, but let's just say that in Victorian England, cognitive behavioural therapy was not widely available.

The nine symptoms used to diagnose borderline personality disorder are:

A fear of abandonment.

Unstable relationships.

Unclear self-image.

Impulsive behaviours.

Self-harm.

Extreme emotional swings.

Chronic feelings of emptiness.

Explosive anger.

Feeling out of touch with reality.

All nine of these symptoms were present in Amelia Dyer's behaviour throughout her life to varying degrees.

The fear of abandonment was a massive factor in her family problems in early life, exacerbated by the BPD sufferer's typical response of lashing out dramatically when confronted with the possibility of abandonment. It was an immense factor in her fear of incarceration and time spent in the workhouse; that in her absence, she would lose the family and the relationships that she clung to, and that fear led to the very manipulative behaviours she exhibited in later life as she tried to control everyone around her and keep them beholden to her.

Unstable relationships were also a defining factor in her life. While her first marriage seemed to have been mostly unmarred by troubles, all her other relationships that she had as an adult were tempestuous at best. In truth, it is entirely possible that the only reason we consider her marriage to George Thomas to have been so successful and peaceful compared to all of her other relationships is because there were no witnesses to disabuse this notion while the relationship was in progress; and because Amelia herself looked back on it through rose-tinted glasses.

Unclear self-image is more difficult to define in terms of Amelia Dyer. Though she did seem to go through periods of considering herself irresistibly attractive and monstrously hideous, these were mostly in response to outside factors as opposed to necessarily being representative of her own feelings about herself. Similarly, throughout her life, she seemed to experience a dichotomy of thought in which she was either a completely reprehensible monster who was undeserving of forgiveness for her sins, or completely justified in absolutely everything that she did because of the circumstances that had driven her to it. Saint or sinner, there seemed to be nothing in between. Such extremes are typical of BPD.

When it comes to impulsive behaviours, it can be difficult to discern the wheat from the chaff. Some of the actions that Amelia Dyer took were doubtless impulsive and, in all likelihood, the very first murder that she committed would have been in response to an overwhelming outburst of explosive anger driving her to permanently silence one of the children in her care. Yet there were also impulsive behaviours in her life that could have been deliberate and calculated moves to throw people off her trail. Much of her 'irrational' behaviour when it came to the courtroom, for instance, was almost certainly theatre intended to support her insanity defence. Yet there were genuine moments where her life would have been made much easier if she had been less impulsive. Her eventual capture and the attention that she drew while living in Reading were almost entirely a result of her impulsively taking on too many babies at once when she could easily have maintained a slow and steady pace. There was no desperate need for a sudden influx of money, she was simply acting on impulse.

While some of her suicide attempts may have been staged as a way to escape justice, at least one was a serious attempt at self-harm. When she consumed two full bottles of laudanum, there was no way that she had enough medical expertise to know that she had built up sufficient immunity to survive it. Even doctors specialising in opiates at the time would not have guessed that someone could survive such a dose, even had they known that person had been inoculating themselves with it for months.

Extreme emotional swings, explosive anger and chronic feelings of emptiness all seemed to go hand in hand, composing the baseline of her experience of life. She would go from happy to miserable at the drop of a hat, from perfectly calm to engulfed in rage. She spent much of her life trying to mask this instability, but those closest to her recognised it and testified to it in court when the time came. They likely thought it was simply an indictment of her character rather than a symptom of a mental illness, but the evidence remains.

As to feeling out of touch with reality; this was perhaps the most defining characteristic of Amelia Dyer. She didn't see anyone else as real. Not in the same way that she was real. Some of them might have been extensions of herself; her children or her husbands, but none of them had internal worlds like she did. This seems like an extreme form of narcissism, but it is not uncommon for people suffering from BPD to feel isolated as they find it difficult to recognise their own experiences in other people. Was Amelia the only one who felt things so deeply and profoundly? Were other people just paper-thin representations of the human experience, all surface with nothing underneath? It justified many of her actions; this belief that she was not only the main character in every story, but that other people weren't even people at all. As we saw with the demonisation of the poor and immoral in Victorian Society; when you stop treating people as people, you can justify any sort of abuse.

Two other common co-morbidities come along with borderline personality disorder: anxiety and substance abuse.

One could argue that anxiety was another of Amelia's defining characteristics and the impetus for many of her actions. She was so afraid of her life being outside of her control that she forcibly took control through acts of violence. It was also the reason that she felt a desperate need to be financially secure. Her propensity for anxiety left her constantly worrying about money, even when her financial situation did not warrant her concern. She then used that worry to justify whatever terrible action she deemed necessary.

As to substance abuse, we know that Amelia indulged heavily in alcohol and drugs throughout her life. Initially as a sort of anaesthetic against the pain of the awful things that she was seeing and doing, and later out of addiction and the persistent self-destructive impulses that BPD produce.

In short, while it is not possible to diagnose a historical person with a modern mental illness, all of the various traits that would have been used in a diagnosis of borderline personality disorder track perfectly with the story of her life.

Setting aside the role of her mental illness, her role as a reaper of society's unwanted, and her role in the social progress that was made as a result of her awful actions; one irrefutable fact remains. Amelia Dyer was not forced to do any of the things that she did. She chose to do those things. She heard about an immoral opportunity to make money, and she took the idea and ran with it. Taking what was already a shady business and pushing it to its most gruesome extreme. Whether she felt that society was encouraging her to commit her crimes, whether her decisions were influenced by her mental illness, or whether her addictions to drugs and alcohol muddied her decision-making to the point that she could justify anything to herself; the fact remains that she chose to kill those children so that she could profit from their deaths, and it is difficult to come up with any childhood trauma, diagnosis or excuse for that beyond the fact that she was an evil person who chose to do evil again and again, because it benefited her.

Want More?

Did you enjoy *The Baby Farm Murders* and want some more True Crime?

YOUR FREE BOOK IS WAITING

From bestselling author Ryan Green

There is a man who is officially classed as "**Britain's most dangerous prisoner**"

The man's name is Robert Maudsley, and his crimes earned him the nickname "**Hannibal the Cannibal**"

This free book is an exploration of his story...

 **nook** **kobo** **iBooks**

★★★★★ *"Ryan brings the horrifying details to life. I can't wait to read more by this author!"*

Get a free copy of **Robert Maudsley: Hannibal the Cannibal** when you sign up to join my Reader's Group.

www.ryangreenbooks.com/free-book

Every Review Helps

If you enjoyed the book and have a moment to spare, I would really appreciate a short review on Amazon. Your help in spreading the word is gratefully received and reviews make a huge difference to helping new readers find me. Without reviewers, us self-published authors would have a hard time!

Type in your link below to be taken straight to my book review page.

US	geni.us/FarmUS
UK	geni.us/FarmUK
Australia	geni.us/FarmAUS
Canada	geni.us/FarmCAN

Thank you! I can't wait to read your thoughts.

About Ryan Green

Ryan Green is a true crime author who lives in Herefordshire, England with his wife, three children, and two dogs. Outside of writing and spending time with his family, Ryan enjoys walking, reading and windsurfing.

Ryan is fascinated with History, Psychology and True Crime. In 2015, he finally started researching and writing his own work and at the end of the year, he released his first book on Britain's most notorious serial killer, Harold Shipman.

He has since written several books on lesser-known subjects, and taken the unique approach of writing from the killer's perspective. He narrates some of the most chilling scenes you'll encounter in the True Crime genre.

You can sign up to Ryan's newsletter to receive a free book, updates, and the latest releases at:

WWW.RYANGREENBOOKS.COM

More Books by Ryan Green

In 1978, Cheryl Bradshaw was a contestant on the popular TV matchmaking show, 'The Dating Game'. From a lineup of eligible bachelors, she selected the handsome daredevil photographer, Rodney Alcala.

As the charmed audience watched the couple embrace, a chilling truth lurked behind the camera lens. Rodney Alcala was a serial killer in the midst of a chilling rampage. Hiding in plain sight.

Alcala lured in his victims by offering them the chance to be a part of his professional photography portfolio, with the promise of launching their modelling careers. But the 1,020 photographs, later found in a secret storage locker by the police, revealed a devastating ulterior motive.

Smile is a chilling account of Rodney Alcala, one of the most prolific serial killers in American history. Ryan Green gives a suspenseful narrative that draws the reader into the real-life horror experienced by the victims with all the elements of a captivating thriller

More Books by Ryan Green

Prostitutes and animals could no longer satisfy Peter Kürten's sexual deviancy. During a burglary of a local tavern, he stumbled upon a nine-year-old girl asleep in her bed. He strangled her, slashed her throat with a pocket knife, and orgasmed upon hearing her blood drip to the floor.

His crimes were halted by World War I and an eight-year prison sentence but he unleashed his urges with a spate of brutal murders in 1929 earning him the nickname "The Düsseldorf Monster".

No one was safe. He committed ferocious attacks, sexual assaults and murder against men, women and children. He used blunt objects, sharp implements or his bare hands, before drinking their blood for sexual satisfaction.

The Monster Within is a chilling account of Peter Kurten, one of the most terrifying serial killers in true crime history. Ryan Green's riveting narrative draws the reader into the real-live horror experienced by the victims and has all the elements of a classic thriller.

More Books by Ryan Green

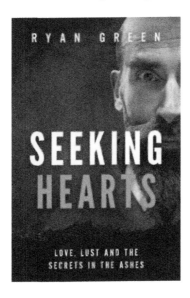

When Inspector Belin set out to catch the elusive Henri Landru for embezzlement and fraud, he wasn't prepared for the complex web of secrets that would unravel.

As war raged on and husbands fought on distant battlefields, Landru preyed upon the vulnerable hearts of lonely young women, presenting himself as a grieving widower desperate to fill the void in his shattered life.

Beneath the façade of a broken man lay a disturbing truth - a predator driven by insatiable desires. Would some of Landru's 283 targets find out in time to save themselves?

Seeking Hearts is a chilling journey through the depths of human darkness. As the riveting tale unfolds, it forces readers to confront the unsettling realisation that, for Henri Landru, murder became the ultimate means of tying up loose ends.

More Books by Ryan Green

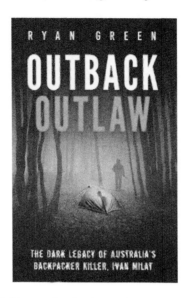

"He was going to kill somebody from the age of 10. It was built into him... I knew he was on a one-way trip. I knew that it was just a matter of how long." - Boris Milat, Ivan's brother

Detaining a man like Ivan Milat would be a monumental challenge. His obsession with firearms and hatred of state power were a highly volatile combination. Sending just a couple of men would result in two dead officers and a prime suspect on the run.

Outback Outlaw is an unflinching and uncompromising account of a man forever cemented in the annals of Australian true crime. Ryan Green's riveting narrative draws the reader into the real-life horror experienced by the victim and has all the elements of a classic thriller.

Free True Crime Audiobook

Printed in Great Britain
by Amazon

61426545R00078